INDIAN MONEYLENDERS AT WORK

SOUTH ASIA INSTITUTE
NEW DELHI BRANCH
HEIDELBERG UNIVERSITY

South Asia Series XIV

INDIAN MONEYLENDERS AT WORK

Case Studies of the Traditional Rural Credit Market in Dhanbad District, Bihar

HANS-DIETER ROTH

Foreword by
DIETMAR ROTHERMUND

MANOHAR
2007

First published 1983
First paperback edition 2007

ISBN 81-7304-730-8

Published by
Ajay Kumar Jain for
Manohar Publishers & Distributors
4753/23, Ansari Road, Daryaganj
New Delhi 110 002

Printed at
Lordson Publishers Pvt. Ltd.
Delhi 110 007

To

Ulrike, Alexander, Tina and Isabel

Foreword

Indian moneylenders have once more extended their operations in recent years. In the 1970s and 1980s institutional credit had proliferated in the countryside, but the reform period after 1991 witnessed a drastic contraction of rural credit. Critics have called it "credit starvation". At the same time the number of operational holdings has about doubled in India from 1970 to 2000 while the total cultivated area has remained the same. This implies a rapid growth of the number of dwarfholders who are bound to get indebted. Market forces have penetrated rural India. Sometimes they have emitted the wrong signals. For instance, when cotton prices rose in the mid 1990s, many peasants started planting cotton although the soil of their holdings was not suitable for it. When the harvest failed some of these peasants committed suicide. In recent years this new phenomenon of rural suicides has spread. In general, moneylenders would strive to keep their debtors alive as they can expect no returns from the dead. But obviously they have not been able to prevent rash acts committed in utter despair.

The nominal interest rates charged by moneylenders are usually exorbitant. They are designed so as to keep the debtors in permanent debt bondage. The effective interest rates are variable. The moneylenders adjust them to the results of the harvest, the personal conditions of the debtor etc. Nevertheless, debt service remains a terrible burden. The peasants are exploited while the moneylenders prospers. The availability of institutional credit was supposed to remove this stranglehold. But often this credit was accessible only to richer peasants and its institutional base was undermined by populist politicians who promised to cancel debts after winning elections. Institutional rural credit thus became a another type of subsidy which the advocates of economic reform wished to curtail. Moreover, the success of micro-credit as demonstrated by Mohammend Yunus and his Grameen Bank in Bangladesh seemed to show that rural credit could be managed in different ways. But it proved to be impossible to satisfy the demand for rural credit in India in this way. Accordingly the type of micro-credit managed by moneylenders has returned to the Indian countryside with a vengeance.

Hans-Dieter Roth's pioneering study of "Indian Moneylenders at Work" is thus once more of great relevance. The fieldwork for this study was done in Dhanbad District, Bihar, in 1970/71. Roth was amazingly successful in getting information from the moneylenders who freely talked about their work to him as he was a German scholar who would obviously not compete with them in their business. Since the basic practices of the moneylenders have not changed, Roth's study is "evergreen" and this new printing is highly welcome.

University of Heidelberg
Germany

Dietmar Rothermund, Ph.D., FRHistS
Professor Emeritus of South Asian History

Preface to the Second Printing

The present study is an enlarged reproduction of a section from my thesis "Institutional Credit and Traditional Debt Relations" which was published in German in 1978 by the south Asia Institute of the University of Heidelberg under the South Asia Series.

To cover a larger circle of readers, particularly in India, it was thought desirable to have at least a part of this thesis translated into English, more so, since the aspects of traditional moneylending and the resulting debt relations are still very important.

My thanks are due to Prof. D. Rothermund of the South Asia Institute, University of Heidelberg, for his invaluable support and for encouraging me to undertake this English language translation, as also for writing the foreword with his profound insights, to the second printing of the book.

I also wish to thank Mr Paras Nath Chaudhary, Mr Ambastha, Mohan Singh and Mr Jha who conducted the extensive fieldwork and surveys in the villages for collecting data and statistical inputs. Last but not least, I cannot help paying my sincerest thanks to the countless villagers who willingly responded to my questions. They really made my task so much easier and without their unstinted cooperation and willingless to help me, this study would not have been possible.

Stuttgart, Germany
February 2007

Hans-Dieter Roth

Contents

List of Tables

Tables in the Text

Tables in the Appendix

List of Sketch

Introduction

Institutional credit programmes supported by governments and often launched on a very wide scale incurring heavy financial expenditure, unfortunately, in many instances, have not achieved their objectives and failed to fulfil the expectations of their clients, who are mostly underprivileged peasants. This is very much true in a country like India, where, in spite of a relatively extensive network of credit institutions, it has so far not been possible to eliminate, or minimise decisively, the predominance of traditional credit activities, particularly the unscrupulous business practices of village moneylenders.

A series of investigations revealed that the credit activities of institutional sources (cooperative banks and rural credit cooperatives supported by the government) have successively increased their share of business in the overall Indian agricultural credit market, especially during the last two decades. However, considering the objectives of these credit institutions, the successes achieved hitherto are not satisfactory.

According to the All-India Rural Credit Survey conducted in 1951-52, the share of credit institutions at the agricultural credit market was 7.3%, out of which 2.9% was loans handled by credit cooperatives, which are the major source of institutional credit. Nearly 70% of all agricultural loans were given by traditional moneylenders. In the year 1961-62 the situation improved somewhat, when the share of cooperative agricultural credits increased to 13.8% Nevertheless, private moneylenders still enjoyed the lion's share in the agricultural credit market amounting to 46.6% of all farming loans.[1]

According to the most recent data, approximately 35% of agricultural

1. Reserve Bank of India, *Report of the All-India Rural Credit Review Committee*, Bombay, 1969, p. 100.

loans were given by cooperative credit institutions.[2] Thus, it can be assumed that traditional credit-givers continue to be predominant in the agricultural credit system in India.[3] The percentage of 35% attributed to cooperative lending institutions is not satisfactory, particularly in view of the fact that these credit agencies were established with the initial objective of curbing the influential position of village moneylenders in order to reduce the traditional indebtedness of Indian farmers.[4] Keeping this objective in mind, it is quite obvious that the cooperative credit system in India has failed to fulfil the function assigned to it in the manner expected.

A series of problems arise from the very strong and unabated position of the circle of traditional moneylenders consisting of large-scale farmers who already have a dominant status in agricultural society and who provided the initial impulse for this study.

Exorbitant interest charges are a common characteristic of traditional moneylender loans A continuous process of granting and repayment of loans, mostly for consumption, creates a chain of transactions, which in turn merely causes an income redistribution in the farming sector of a country like India. The outcome of this process is, as a rule, in favour of the large-scale farmers.

If the farm-households are classified into two groups, one consisting of debtors (small farmers) and the other consisting of creditors (big farmers), a permanent process of income transfers can be observed taking place through the mechanism of continuous borrowing and settlement of loans at high interest rates. The extent of such income transfers is considerably high. On the basis of empirical surveys on agriculture in India prior to 1960, which even today has traditional characteristics, it can be assumed that at an average about 90% of the regular income from agriculture (usually in the form of kind) is utilized for recurrent consumption. Nor is the remaining 10% used for capital formation and/or

2. C.D. Datey, "Cooperative Credit" in *Cooperative News Digest*, Vol. XXV, No. 12, December 1974, Reserve Bank of India, Agricultural Credit Department, p. 179

3. According to my own findings, the predominance of traditional credit-givers is even more distinct, because the institutional credit agencies handle a share of only 19.2% of the overall credit transactions in the case villages (See Appendix, Table A-1).

4. ". . .the cooperative movement was initiated in the country for safeguarding the interests of the small farmers and to save them from the clutches of the moneylenders." C. Subramanium, "Co-ops only Alternative to Moneylenders" in *Cooperative News Digest*, Vol. XXVII, No. 12, December 1976, Reserve Bank of India, p. 178. "The land mortgage banks in India were started . . . with the main objective of saving the farmers from losing their land on account of their inability to meet their debts to the moneylenders."

productive purposes; nearly 60% of this is utilized either for loan-repayments or lending. Presuming that borrowings and repayments are equal, which may however not necessarily be correct, then the process of income redistribution in Indian agriculture would cover just about 3% of the regular agricultural production.[5]

Under traditional debt relations this study covers all credit transactions between private moneylenders (creditors) and village households (debtors). These can be either pure loan obligations or even personal dependency relationships as well as a combination of both forms. Here we will limit ourselves to a detailed analysis of the traditional credit markets in three selected case-villages (which is an excerpt from a comprehensive study conducted by the author covering all aspects of agricultural credit systems, both traditional and institutional) in the district of Dhanbad, Bihar, India.[6]

The main issue of the present analysis is to ascertain the potential for an agricultural surplus production and also the typification of traditional credit market forms. Typification of the market form concerning supply enables us to make important conclusions on the degree of influence of traditional village moneylenders and on the structure of prevailing interest rates. Interest charges of traditional moneylender-loans, which are usually very high, are discussed in detail since heavy interest rates not only create debt obligations but are also meant to establish dependency relations of a long-term nature. A description of actual forms of debt relations is presented thereafter with examples of interest siphoning mechanisms practiced by moneylenders in the case-villages. The final part illustrates the various traditional forms of transfer of property rights, which frequently are the inevitable outcome of previous debt commitments, and their detrimental socio-economic effects on small farm households.

Selection of Case-Villages

The specific features of the traditional credit market are presented here on the basis of the findings from case studies of three selected villages in the Dhanbad district, which enabled us to make an analysis of the traditional credit system. Though the survey was not conducted in accordance with the strict requirements of a representative random selection, certain major criteria which were also characteristics of other villages in the case-area had to be observed. Hence, the findings of this study can be

5. W. von Urff, "Agrarpolitische Probleme der Entwicklungslaender", *Vorlesungsmanuskript*, Heidelberg, 1972, p. 4.

6. H.D. Roth, *Institutioneller Agrarkredit und traditionelle Schuldverhaeltnisse*, Wiesbaden, 1978.

applied to villages—with certain limitations—which have the same or similar structural features as the case-villages.

It was necessary to assume that the traditional agricultural credit system particularly cannot be studied without taking into consideration the situation of land ownership, caste and social structures and the resulting power structures in the villages. Therefore, the selection of case-villages was done in such a manner so as to include villages having different conditions of ownership, caste and social spectrums. This selection was particularly relevant because the case area had earlier been a tribal region where a socio-economic evolution took place due to the alien infiltration of Hindus and traders during the 19th century. This influx destroyed the system of tribal agriculture and also created new rural social structures and settlement-type villages. In the selection of case-villages for this study, due consideration was given to this socio-historical development in the area under survey by taking into account villages with relatively uniform ethnical structures and uniform distribution of land, as well as villages where there was a strong polarisation of land ownership and consequently a polarisation of the caste structure. A characteristic of the first type of village is the absence of Hindu farmers with high social status while the latter type consists of villages where the Hindu caste hierarchy is deeply established as a social order. The second type of village is, therefore, marked by a strong stratification among inhabitants who belong to social groups ranging from high to low status, dominated by a group of Hindu landlords who are socially, economically, and partly also numerically superior.[7]

Description of Case-Villages

KATHWARI/VILLAGE 1

Comprising of 59 households Kathwari is the largest of the three case villages; it is situated in the agricultural hinterland in the southern part of the case area.[8] It belongs administratively to the Chas Block and is the furthest away, about 40 km. from the district centre of Dhanbad. It is connected to the township of Pindrajora, situated near the main trunk road Dhanbad-Purulia, by a *kaccha* road of 5 km. Most households in Kathwari village visit the weekly market in Pindrajora for their requirements. The road, however, can be used during the rainy season only by a jeep, a tonga or by an ox-cart. The credit cooperative situated in

7. E. Schmitt, "Die bevoelkerungsgeschichtliche Entwicklung im Dhanbad-Distrikt seit der Kolonialisierung, Eine zusammenfassende Darstellung der Detribalisierung", SFB 16, Dhanbad-Projekt, unveroeff. Manuskript, He delberg, 1974.

8. See Sketch 1 for location of case-villages.

Pindrajora covers Kathwari village but has now ceased to function. Thus Village 1, as we shall refer to Kathwari for convenience, represents one of the villages where there is no institutional agricultural credit agency.

The main agricultural crop in this village (as in other villages) is paddy, which is still cultivated according to traditional methods and primarily for self-consumption. All households have their own paddy-land. Land tenure is not practiced in this village. The village has no artificial irrigation system; the entire paddy cultivation is rain fed.

Nearly 90% of farms in Kathwari village are under the size of 5.0 Standard Acres.[9] There are only 5 farms in the size-category of 5.0—10.0 Standard Acres and one larger than 10.0 (see Table 1). The moneylending households consist of farmers who own these larger farms. As seen in Table 3 this village, situated in the agricultural hinterland of the case-area, has the most balanced distribution of land among all the villages under study.

The inhabitants of Kathwari belong to different castes. The village community is, therefore, multi-ethnic as are most of the settlements in this region. As mentioned earlier, the peculiar socio-historic development of the case-area has created two kinds of villages or settlement types. On one hand, there are villages where the indigenous social structure has remained partly intact because of the absence of high status Hindu farmers. On the other hand, there are villages where the tribal social structure was displaced and superseded by a Hindu social order. These villages are dominated by a socially superior group of Hindu landowners.[10]

Despite the presence of a Brahmin population in this village, the Hindu caste hierarchy has not penetrated the village society and established itself as a social order. These Brahmin households are economically and socially insignificant. Therefore, Village 1, typifies a rural society where the tribal social structure has remained almost intact and, last but not least, also due to the domination of the Kurmi Mahatos group. The Kurmi Mahatos caste is numerically the strongest community in this village and is constituted of a group of former tribals. They are the largest tribal group who have successfully become Hindus and have gained a respectable socio-economic status in the district, particularly those Kurmi Mahatos who settled in the agricultural hinterland were able to change over to intensive farming and establish themselves socially in the wake of the changes in the socio-economic conditions. The most decisive socio-structural feature in Village 1 is, hence, the fact that castes having

9. Standard Acre—A comparative measure of land deduced on the basis of differences in soil fertilities. See Section Sampling Method, Standardisation of Area Units, p. 12.

10. E. Schmitt, "Die bevoelkerungsgeschichtliche Entwicklung. . .", op. cit., pp. 54, 55.

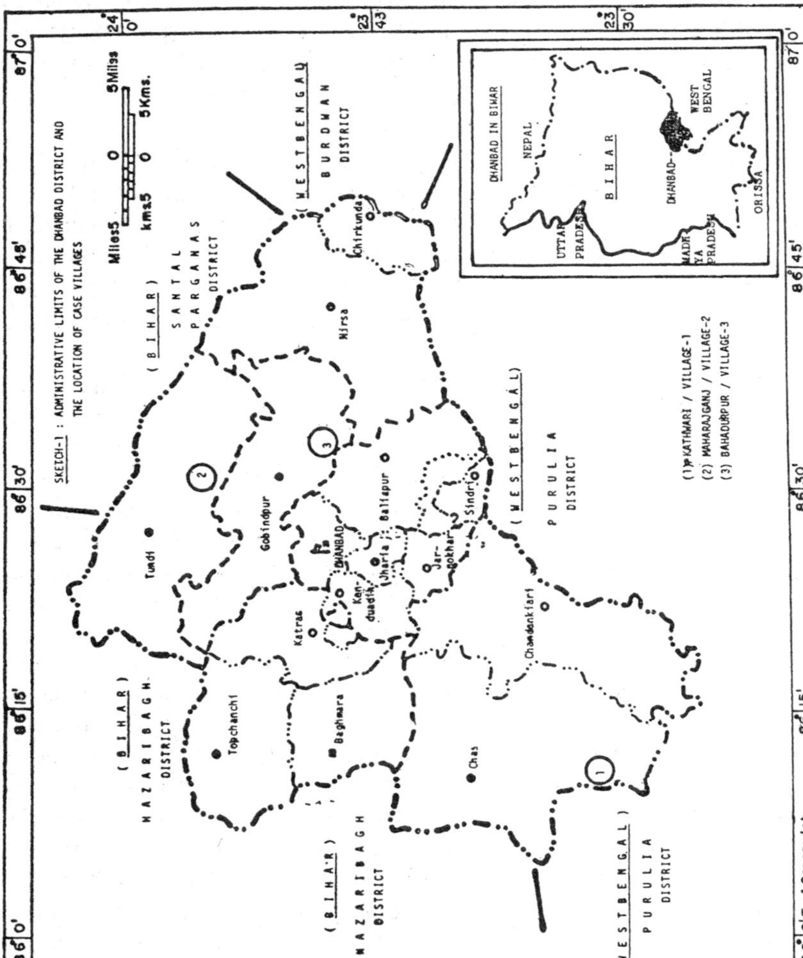
SKETCH-1 : ADMINISTRATIVE LIMITS OF THE DHANBAD DISTRICT AND THE LOCATION OF CASE VILLAGES
(1) KATHWARI / VILLAGE-1
(2) MAHARAJGANJ / VILLAGE-2
(3) BAHADURPUR / VILLAGE-3
(BIHAR) SANTAL PARGANAS DISTRICT
(WEST BENGAL) BURDWAN DISTRICT
(WEST BENGAL) PURULIA DISTRICT
(BIHAR) HAZARIBAGH DISTRICT
DHANBAD IN BIHAR
NEPAL
BIHAR
UTTAR PRADESH
MADHYA PRADESH
WEST BENGAL
ORISSA
DHANBAD
Tundi
Gobindpur
Nirsa
Chirkunda
Baliapur
Sindri
Jharia
Katras
Topchanchi
Baghmara
Chas
Chandankiari
86°0'E of Greenwich

different status are socially independent; they have settled in close proximity with each other and they enjoy equal rights. The hierarchical social structure of this village, which would imply a unilateral dependence on the superior Hindu caste, is not existent in this village despite the presence of 7 Brahmin households.

TABLE 1

Farm Size Structure in the Case Villages (in StA)*

	Under 2.0		2.01 to 5.0		5.01 to 10.0		Over 10 0		Total	
	No.	%	No.	%	No.	%	No.	%	No.	%
Village 1	26	44.1	27	45.7	05	08.5	01	01.7	59	100
Village 2	26	86.7	03	10.0	—	—	01	03.3	30	100
Village 3	10	32.2	11	35.5	07	22.6	03	09.7	31	100
Total	62	51.6	41	34.2	12	10.0	05	04.2	120	100

Remark: * StA : Standard Acre—A comparative measure of land area deduced on the basis of differences in soil fertilities. See Section 'Standardisation of Area-Units.'

Source : Own Surveys.

Being situated in the agricultural hinterland of the case-area, there are practically no other sources of income in Village 1 besides agriculture. Therefore, very few households have any supplementary off-farm earnings. Besides 3 farm workers, who are permanently employed in other farms in the village, there are only 10 households which have any regular additional income. They work either in the township of Chas (Bokaro-Steel, Public Service) or are engaged in traditional rural handicrafts (wickerwork, tailoring, etc.). Therefore, Village 1 has the least number of households out of all the case villages, which have regular off-farm earnings (see Table 2).

MAHARAJGANJ/VILLAGE 2

In relation to other villages in the case area Maharajganj has a special position because it is situated along a state highway. It is about 30 km from the district centre, Dhanbad, and belongs to the Tundi Block, which forms the northern boundary of the case-area, and has the most developed infrastructure of all villages. Another significant difference is the presence of a credit cooperative established in 1930 which is one of the oldest credit cooperatives in the district. The cooperative in Maharajganj functions well.

Being centrally situated along the main trunk road, Dhanbad-Tundi-Giridih (the only connection between Dhanbad district and the neighbouring district of Hazaribagh), it has emerged as a transit stop for omnibuses plying on this route. Maharajganj is also a marketing centre covering a relatively large area of farm settlements. This, however, has not prompted the villagers, who cultivate small land-holdings which are inadequate even for self-subsistence, to give up farming; rather they have combined both agricultural and non-agricultural occupations.

TABLE 2

Households with Members having Permanent Off Farm Income Sources

Village/ farm size class (in StA)	Number of households	Farm labourers	Coal mining industries	Public services	Handicrafts, retail trade and other service-occupations	Total
Village—1						
Under 2.0	26	03	03	—	—	06
2 01— 5.0	27	—	01	01	01	03
5 01—10.0	05	—	—	01	01	02
Over 10.0	01	—	—	01	01	02
Total	59	03	04	03	03	13
Village—2						
Under 2 0	26	05	02	03	12	22
2.01— 5.0	03	—	—	01	02	03
5.01—10.0	—	—	—	—	—	—
Over 10.0	01	—	-	01	01	02
Total	30	05	02	05	15	27
Village—3						
Under 2.0	10	04	02	—	—	06
2.01— 5.0	11	02	02	01	—	05
5.01—10.0	07	—	01	07	03	11
Over 10.0	03	—	—	04	02	06
Total	31	06	05	12	05	28
All Villages	120	14	11	20	23	68

Source : Own Surveys.

Although the primary occupation in Village 2 is still agriculture, there are many households earning additional incomes from off-farm occupations, such as retail trade, processing agricultural produce, or providing traditional craft services. At the time of this study, at least 27 out of the 30 village households had off-farm incomes; for example, the informal village chief, the Mukhiya, had several business ventures such as a rice mill, textile trade and the sale of sundry goods. This helped the

TABLE 3

Caste Structure and Land Ownership Distribution in Case Villages

			Village (1)	Village (2)	Village (3)	Total
Upper Castes	Number of Households	No.	7	—	12	19
		%	11.9	—	38.7	15.8
	Share of Agr. Land	Qty.	12.9	—	102.5	115.4
		%	7.8	—	74.4	33.2
Backward Castes	Number of Households	No.	41	20*	1	62
		%	69.5	66.7	3.2	51.7
	Share of Agr. Land	Qty.	130.6	37.6**	4.0	172.2
		%	79.3	82.6	2.9	49.5
Sched. Castes	Number of Households	No.	—	10+	12	22
		%	—	33.3	38.7	18.3
	Share of Agr. Land	Qty.	—	7.9	13.7	21.6
		%	—	17.4	9.9	6.2
Sched. Tribes	Number of Households	No.	5	—	6	11
		%	8.4	—	19.4	9.2
	Share of Agr. Land	Qty.	8.6	—	17.6	26.2
		%	5.2	—	12.8	7.5
Muslims	Number of Households	No.	6	—	—	6
		%	10.2	—	—	5.0
	Share of Agr. Land	Qty.	12.6	—	—	12.6
		%	7.7	—	—	3.6
Total	Number of Households	No.	59	30	31	120
		%	100	100	100	100
	Share of Agr. Land	Qty.	164.7	45.5	137.8	348.0
		%	100	100	100	100

Remarks : *Including three landless households.
**Out of this, 18.2 StA amounting to 40.0% of the agricultural land in the village belong to the Mukhyia of the village.
+Including one landless (Farm Labourer) household.

Source : Own Surveys.

villagers to find alternative sources of income. The Mukhiya belongs to the merchant caste of Baniya, and is a dominating figure in the village both economically and socially. He is the owner of the only large farm in the village and functions also as the secretary of the cooperative as well as the postmaster. This is a classic example of the accumulation of official and social functions.

Village 2 has the most unequal distribution of land out of all three case villages. Almost 40% of arable land belongs to the Mukhiya's family. Thus, besides his other business ventures and official functions, the Mukhiya is also the only employer in the village. The remaining 60% of land is distributed among 96.7% of village households, consisting of backward castes (Sonar, Teli, Mandal) having medium to low social status or to scheduled castes (Rajwar) with very low social status. The Rajwars are numerically the strongest scheduled caste in the villages of the case-area. They are former tribals who later became Hindus. In contrast to the Kurmi Mahatos, the Rajwars could not hold their own socially or economically against the Hindus and traders who migrated during the 19th century. Thus, they failed to transform themselves as Hindus as positively as their former tribal neighbours, the Kurmi Mahatos. Therefore, the Rajwars are socio-economically in the lowest category of scheduled castes. They, and also the Gathwars of Village 3, work as farm labourers.

While Village 1 is dominated socially as well as numerically by the Kurmi Mahatos and Village 3 is dominated by a group of Hindu landlords, Village 2 is controlled by a single family belonging to the merchant caste of Baniya. The Baniyas are also an alien group of migrants like the Hindu landowners. It can, therefore, be presumed that the Mukhiya's family continuously built up its dominating position by acquiring land and venturing into business activities through exploitary means. Here, Schmitt identifies essentially two alien groups who have become rich and powerful by exploiting the tribals. Besides Hindu farmers and landowners, they are mainly the traders and merchants who have compelled the tribals to bonded labour by creating debt obligations.[11]

BAHADURPUR/VILLAGE 3

Bahadurpur is situated in Govindpur Block about 22 km from the district capital of Dhanbad. Like Village 1, it has no direct road connection and is accessible during the rainy season only by a jeep, an ox-cart, or by a tonga.

11. E. Schmitt, "Die bevoelkerungsgeschichtliche Entwicklung. . .", op. cit., pp. 19, 20.

As Table 3 demonstrates, the entire spectrum of caste groups in the case-area (ranging from the castes with the highest social prestige such as Brahmins, Bhumihars to Non-Hindu Santals down to the lowest scheduled castes of Rajwars and Gathwars) is represented in Village 3. Those belonging to upper castes are descendants of a Hindu landowner-group which migrated during the 19th century. They had the rights of Zamindars during the earlier days and actually are the founders of the village.[12] When the village was established by the ancestors of the upper caste households, the lower caste groups were brought in and settled in the village purposely to provide the labour requirements of the Hindu landowners. Evidence supporting this historical development of the village can be found still in the bonded labour commitments between even the third generation of upper castes and scheduled castes or tribes.

Farms over the size of 5.0 Standard Acres are usually owned by upper caste households (farms below 5.0 are exceptional) while the scheduled castes and tribals cultivate smaller farms. Corresponding to the farm-size structure, the distribution of land in this village is extremely unequal. As Table 3 shows, 102.5 Standard Acres of land or 74.4% of the total arable land belong to 12 upper caste households. In relation to this, the nineteen underprivileged caste households (corresponding to 61.3% of village households) own a little over one-fourth of the farm land. However, the situation of scheduled tribes with regard to land-ownership is much better than that of the scheduled castes.

Village 3 typifies a sample case with a polarisation of land ownership and a parallel polarisation of the caste structure. Besides, it is also a fine example of a settlement type, where the Hindu caste hierarchy is deeply entrenched and established as a social order. A characteristic feature of this village is the strongly stratified character of the population in which social groups of both low and high status are dominated by a group of Hindu landlords who are economically as well as numerically superior implying strong socio-economic dependencies among the underprivileged groups.

Contrary to a village community living together in harmony free of social dependencies such as village 1, village 3 illustrates a settlement with a social and cultural separation of different groups. Communities are strictly separated according to castes (Tolas) resulting in social segregation in this village. This type of settlement necessarily implies a unilateral dependency of the underprivileged groups on the dominating upper castes.

Bahadurpur had a credit cooperative which suspended operations

12. D. Rothermund, D.C. Wadhwa (ed.). *Zamindars, Mines and Peasants*, South Asian Studies, No. IX (a), New Delhi, 1978.

after the revenue year 1969/70. Key positions in this cooperative were occupied mainly by persons belonging to the upper castes in this village as well as some from neighbouring village.

Research Methodology and Data Collection

After the selection of case villages, it was necessary to acquaint the villagers with the topic of the study and to introduce the research-questionnaire. For this purpose, assistance from suitable key persons (Teachers, Panches) was obtained. The villages were visited frequently in order to pre-test the questionnaire which was later modified several times according to the reactions of the respondents. In its final version, the questionnaire met the requirements of a rational evaluation of data collection.

A complete coverage of all three case villages comprising a total of 120 households was undertaken. The questionnaire was given to a list of pre-arranged households. An exhaustive coverage was essential since the objective of the study was to evaluate and analyse all aspects of the traditional credit markets as deeply and extensively as possible. All credit procedures within a period of 6 years were covered in detail in order to illustrate the changes in the process of credit supply chronologically.

Since decisions in credit transactions are usually taken by the chief householder, the interviews were conducted with the head of the family. The services of three Indian Research Assistants were obtained by the author in conducting this study. They were all well experienced and qualified in research field-work and were also proficient in the different dialects of the languages spoken in the case-area.

Sampling Method, Standardisation of Area Units, Terminological Limitations

Based on the fact that all sample households covered in this study have their own land, with the exception of four households in Village 3, the terms 'farm' and 'household' are used as a unit and, therefore, are identical in meaning. Production and consumption are interrelated because, on one hand, the food supply of the household is mainly derived from the yield which is jointly brought in and, on the other, the man-power needs of the farm are covered from the labour pool of family members. Therefore, the terms 'farm' and 'household' refer to a group of persons related to each other who cultivate their own land and also utilize the yields collectively.

To meet the requirements of a correct comparison of farms, differences in quality and fertility of paddy lands mainly due to the varying degrees of water seepage of the top soil, were standardised by converting to the comparative area unit of 'Standard Acre' (StA). Based on the average yields of different soil qualities, the conversion coefficients are:

Bahal	—	1.0
Kanali	—	0.8
Baid	—	0.6
Gora	—	1.0
Tanr	—	0.4

All data regarding land given in this study are related to the total extent of land belonging to a farm. Unless otherwise mentioned, the area unit for land is in Standard Acres (StA).

The households sampled on the basis of land ownership are grouped:

Under		2.0 StA
2.01	—	5.0 StA
5.01	—	10.0 StA
over		10.0 StA

For the purpose of terminological limitations, farms under 2.0 Standard Acres are categorised as 'Marginal' farms and those between 2.01 and 5.0 Standard Acres are termed as 'Small' farms. When considered together, these two categories represented the 'Problem Farms' within the framework of this study. Farms belonging to this category are faced with the problem of securing an adequate income from agriculture. This is, however, an arbitrary grouping, since farms under 2.0 Standard Acres are obviously not in a position to support a family of five to six persons from cultivation alone. Despite this rather unrealistic, or less realistic grouping, the term 'Problem Farms' had to be retained, since both farm categories have similar problems and also because the subsistence threshold for a five to six member family is in the upper scale of this farm group, that is at about 4 Acres.[13]

According to conditions prevailing in the case-area and in the case villages, farms over 10.0 Standard Acres are classified as 'Large' farms

13. A similar conclusion is made in a survey conducted in a neighbouring district having comparative farm size structures and very similar agricultural prerequisites. W. van Urff, W. Jopich, H. Stephan, "Zur Durchfuehrbarkeit eines deutsch-indischen Landwirtschaftsprojektes im Distrikt Ranchi (Indien)". Gutachten erstellt im *Auftrag des Bundesministeriums fuer wirtschaftliche Zusammenarbeit*, Heidelberg, 1972.

and those between 5.01 to 10.0 Standard Acres are grouped as 'Medium' farms. Following the sub-division of a traditional agriculture into a 'Surplus Section' and a 'Deficit Section' undertaken by Dandekar in his critical comments on Schultz, the group of 'problem farms' is classified under the 'Deficit Section' while the large and medium sized farms are grouped under the 'Surplus Section'.[14]

14. V.M. Dandekar, "Transforming Traditional Agriculture, A Critique of Prof. Schultz" in *Economic and Political Weekly*, August 20, 1966.

CHAPTER I

The Traditional Rural Credit System

The credit market in the area under survey consists of an institutional and a traditional system. The institutional system is organised on a cooperative basis and is supported by the government. The traditional system is related mainly to credit activities of farmers-cum-moneylenders, friends and relatives and, therefore, is organised on private initiative. Thus, the credit market in the case area can be grouped basically into an institutional/organised system and a traditional/unorganised system. In the following presentation the traditional credit system will be studied in detail. The focus will be on the village moneylender as the most important source of credit in the traditional credit system.

The term 'moneylending', which denotes the lending business of village moneylenders, known as Mahajan in the case area, covers cash loans as well as loans in kind, usually in paddy. Considering the fact that the moneylender is also very active in the loan of natural produce, the term 'moneylending' is misleading in the brevity of its connotation. In certain instances, the lending business is combined, involving both cash and kind, so that a loan given in cash (or kind) is settled in kind (or cash). Sometimes, though the loan capital is settled in cash (or kind) the interest is paid in kind (or cash). It was observed in the survey that various combinations of granting and settlement of loans are practiced.

Irrespective of the form of loans (cash or kind) credit activities of village moneylenders can be classified into pure personal loans and loans against mortgages of property titles. While personal loans are given on verbal agreements between the creditor and debtor who jointly decide on the credit conditions, mortgage loans are given against the transfer of a property title to the creditor with the right of use either for a limited or unlimited period.

The Potential to Produce Agricultural Surplus

It can be assumed that the potential for producing an agricultural surplus is determined by the farm and household incomes. Accordingly, a surplus of cash or produce occurs when the household and farm incomes exceed the expenditure needs of the household and the farm. Differences in income levels are related to unequal distribution of land and unequal opportunities to earn supplementary off-farm incomes, mainly due to differences in caste and educational standards.[1]

Table 1.1 shows that the concentration of land-ownership in Village 2 and Village 3 is particularly strong. While 60% of arable land is in farms up to 5 Standard Acres in Village 2 covering 96.7% of all farms in this village, the remaining 40% is cultivated in farms of over 5 Standard Acres covering only 3.3% of the total number of farms. This 40% of land belongs to one single farm managed by the Mukhiya (Chief) of the village. In Village 3 over two-thirds of the farms are below 5 Standard Acres. Nearly one-third of the arable land in this village is cultivated in these farms; 32.3% of farms are larger than 5 Standard Acres and belong exclusively to the higher castes. These farms account for the cultivation of 67.2% of arable land in this village. In Village 1, the distribution of land is relatively uniform. But even here, over one-fourth of arable land belongs to farms over 5 Standard Acres representing 10.2% of farms in this village.

The concentration of agricultural land indicates that the potential for producing an agricultural surplus exists only in the higher farm-size categories covering only a few farms where the potential is further enhanced due to better opportunities for earning supplementary off-farm incomes in cash.

Following the critical remarks by Dandekar on the hypothesis of Schultz, a traditional agriculture of the Schultz-type can be subdivided into two sectors based on the unequal distribution of land.[2] One sector is made up of farms producing an agricultural surplus, whilst the other sector immediately adjacent to it is made up of deficit farms. According to

1. Surveys conducted by the author as well as other parallel investigations have revealed that family members of large and medium scale upper caste farmers enjoy better educational opportunities and, therefore, are at an advantage to gain attractive employment in public service as well as in the mining and industrial sectors. Besides, these farmers or their family members are also actively engaged in trade or are self-employed. E.W. Kropp, "Landwirtschaftliche Kapitalbildung unter Industrie-Einfluss, Ein empirischer Beitrag zum Spar—und Investitionsverhalten landwirtschaftlicher Haushalte in Indien". unveroeff. Manuskript, Heidelberg, 1976, p. 339.

2. V.M. Dandekar, "Transforming Traditional Agriculture, A Critique of Prof. Schultz" in *Economic and Political Weekly*, August 20, 1966, p. 25.

TABLE 1.1

Concentration of Farm Land in Case Villages (in StA)

Farm size class (in StA)	Village 1		Village 2		Village 3		All Villages	
	Percentage of households	Percentage of land area	Percentage of households	Percentage of land area	Percentage of households	Percentage of land area	Percentage of households	Percentage of land area
Up to 2.0	44.1	20.0	86.7	42.8	32.3	06.0	51.7	17.4
Up to 5.0	89.8	73.1	96.7	60.0	67.7	32.8	85.8	55.5
Up to 10.0	98.3	93.7	96.7	60.0	90.3	74.1	95.8	91.6
All Classes	100.0	100.0	100.0	100.0	100.0	100.0	100.0	100.0

Source : Own Surveys.

Dandekar the characteristic difference between these two sectors is the 'Man-Land Ratio'. In relation to productivity and production techniques, however, no significant differences between the surplus and deficit sectors can be identified.[3]

While the surplus sector is less burdened with population resulting in a relatively low man-land ratio and, therefore, has a potential to produce an agricultural surplus, the deficit sector is marked by a relatively high man-land ratio. The corresponding heavy burden of population in the deficit sector could be compensated only through dissaving and capital consumption.[4]

One of the main theories of Schultz that the traditional agriculture is in a state of equilibrium can be applied therefore only to the surplus sector. Due to dissavings and capital consumption this theory is inapplicable to the deficit sector.[5] This is clearly evident from the findings of our surveys and the pattern of financing domestic affairs (see Appendix, Table A6).

Alternative Uses of Agricultural Surplus

The following analysis of alternative uses of agricultural surplus is based on the assumption that the potential for producing a surplus lies mainly in medium and large sized farms which are over 5 Standard Acres. According to the criteria mentioned earlier, these farms belong to the surplus sector while farms below 5 Standard Acres form the deficit sector. This, however, is a highly simplified and arbitrary grouping which does not correspond to the definition of the subsistence threshold of farms around the size of 4 Standard Acres. The method of classifying farm-sizes used in the survey, however, made this grouping unavoidable. Considering

3. "In short, agriculture in the sector which produces a surplus over subsistence is as traditional as agriculture in the other sector which does not produce a surplus." Ibid., p. 33.

4. "Thanks to the very unequal distribution of land among the people dependent on it, there exists a sector within traditional agriculture which is not overburdened with population and which therefore produces a surplus of varying degree over subsistence. Consequently, in the residual sector, the burden of population is all the more excessive and dissaving and disinvestment of varying degree prevail." V.M. Dandekar, "Transforming Traditional Agriculture", op. cit., p. 33.

5. ". . . here traditional agriculture is characterized not by a state of equilibrium but a state of continuous deterioration with negative net saving and investment. Because it does not produce enough for its subsistence, it lives and survives by capital consumption, that is by cheating the land, cheating the cattle and finally cheating the man." V.M. Dandekar, "Transforming Traditional Agriculture", op. cit., p. 35.

the chronic deficit in food and the capital consumption to finance domestic affairs, it is obviously the farms below the size of 5 Standard Acres which belong to the deficit sector. The pattern of financing the most important items of domestic expenditure clearly indicates that agricultural surpluses are insignificant in these farms.[6]

Agricultural surplus is the balance portion of production that remains in the farm and/or household for free disposal after own consumption and meeting the operational expenses of the farm. Cash surpluses of households earned from off-farm incomes are not taken into account in this survey. Production surpluses of farms in the case area are mostly in paddy. Surplus incomes can be used to improve and intensify the production, invest in land, livestock and buildings as well as to finance family events (marriages, funerals), construction of houses, legal proceedings and education of children. Besides these farm and domestic expenses surplus production can also be invested in moneylending and trade.[7]

Following the theory of Schultz, investments to expand the stock of traditional production factors in a traditional agriculture are either not made or made at modest levels. According to Schultz, primarily non-traditional production means are helpful in increasing the production. Considering the high profitability of modern production means, it can be suggested that these are themselves inducements to invest more agricultural surpluses in such production means and techniques to achieve higher production levels. However, the findings of our survey as well as other studies have clearly demonstrated that there has been no intensive increase in the agricultural production in the district of Dhanbad. Agriculture is still in an undeveloped stage. Von Urff states: "Comparing the development of agriculture in the district during the last 10 years, the situation can be interpreted as a relative stagnation."[8]

There are a number of indicators to support this interpretation, such as decline in paddy production, drop in the irrigated agricultural land, decrease in the use of improved seed varieties and low percentage (4%) of multiple cropping. Further, the paddy output per unit area of land increased only by 0.6% per year between 1957-58 and 1965-66.[9] Hence there are no avenues to increase production by bringing more land under paddy cultivation and/or increased paddy yields.

6. See Appendix, Table A6.

7. See Appendix, Tables A2 to A8.

8. W. von Urff, et al., "*Wirtschaftliche und soziale Dualismen in einem indischen Bergbaugebiet*, dargestellt am Beispiel des Distriktes Dhanbad-Bihar. Eine zusammenfassende Darstellung des Forschungsprojektes." SFB 16, unveroeff. Manuskript, Heidelberg, 1972, p. 20.

9. R.N. Maharaj. "The Impact of State Policy on Agricultural Development", SFB 16, Dhanbad-Project, unpublished manuscript, Heidelberg, 1972, p. 5.

The above analysis of the traditional agricultural situation in the case area necessarily leads us to the hypothesis that the agricultural surplus in the surplus sector is used mainly for purposes having no or little effect on agricultural production. If we visualise the situation of agriculture in the area under survey, where parallel to the surplus sector a deficit sector exists with periodic as well as sporadic credit demands for consumption purposes, it is quite clear that meeting this credit demand provides an almost classic and profitable form of investment for agricultural surpluses. While the periodic and, therefore, chronic credit demand arises from the continuous incongruity between income and expenditure, the sporadic credit demand can be explained mainly by crop failures often due to climatic factors and occasional high family expenses such as marriages and funerals. The agricultural surplus thus takes on a vital financial function in that it serves to balance the dearth of capital in the deficit sector with the surplus capital in the surplus sector. The moneylender, being identical with the surplus producer, manages this crucial function.

A rough idea of the use of agricultural surplus in farms over the size of 5 Standard Acres belonging to the surplus sector can be gained from Tables A2 and A8 in the Appendix, where the financing pattern of most of the important items of expenditure is illustrated. A summary of these data, given in Table 1.2, demonstrates that in farms over 5 Standard Acres Rs. 129,730 was incurred as expenditure to finance domestic needs and Rs. 24,767 was invested in farm operations. Considering the amounts separately for domestic and farm expenses, it can be seen that Rs. 87,308 or 67.3% was used for household needs and only Rs. 42,422 or 32.7% for farm operations.[10] This relation indicates clearly that expenditure for domestic needs has a higher priority than that for farm operations. Comparing the value of surplus incomes used for financing domestic and farm expenses, it can be noted that Rs. 15,188 worth of agricultural surplus was utilized for domestic needs while the value of farm expenses amounts to Rs. 9,579.[11] Certain items of expenditure in farm operations such as investments in land and livestock can be considered as productive investments only in specific instances. Generally, such investments only indicate a change of ownership, which could be economically unproductive and socially undesirable. Presuming that the farmer who sells the land belongs to the deficit sector and the buyer belongs to the surplus sector, the change of ownership will not result in an overall increase in production.

10. Circumstances prevailing in the case area made it quite difficult to distinguish between buildings used for living and for farm purposes. Therefore, expenditure incurred in the construction of buildings was equally divided into domestic and farm expenses.

11. See above.

Production will increase only if the land is utilized more intensively in the surplus sector. Since the intensity of land utilization is almost similar in both sectors, the change of ownership merely creates an increased concentration of land in one sector.

Considering the farm investments on the basis of the above aspects, it is evident that production potential can be increased only through investments in land improvement and irrigation as only these investments lead to genuine capital formation. In relation to the total expenditure of these farms, the percentage of such investments is only 12%. Over 60% of such investments are financed through institutional credits at low interest rates and only 22.3% out of surplus production.

Comparing the amount of Rs. 24,767 (value of agricultural surplus used to finance domestic and farm expenditure) with the amount of Rs. 33,492 (value of surplus invested in moneylending) it is clear that an absolutely higher portion of surplus is diverted to lending purposes. Assuming that the lending businesses of farmers engaged in moneylending extend beyond their own village, it is also obvious that priority is given to moneylending as an alternative form of investing agricultural surpluses.

A series of empirically justifiable indicators on the development of agriculture in the case area, together with the comments of Schultz on the investment pattern of traditional farmers, lead us to the conclusion that a major part of surplus production is used for consumption and lending. Commenting on the use of agricultural savings potential Dandekar arrives at almost the same conclusion:

> . . . there are three main channels of investment in which a large part of savings flows: buying or acquiring of additional land for renting out; moneylending for consumption purposes at exorbitant interest rates; and trading and shopkeeping. Poverty and hunger existent in the other sector provide ideal conditions to pursue these activities, and for a competent operator, the returns to investment in these lines far exceed any conceivable returns to even improved inputs in agriculture. Therefore, as investment decisions they are completely justifiable.[12]

A major part of surplus production invested in moneylending (77.7%) is utilized for consumption loans. Therefore, most of the surplus production is used for private consumption without having any decisive impact on the production potential (see Table 1.2). This is a wasteful

12. V.M. Dandekar, "Questions of Economic Analysis and the Consequences of Population Growth, Comment" in *Subsistence Agriculture and Economic Development*, Wharton, Jr., (ed.), Chicago, 1965, p. 374.

TABLE 1.2

Share of Income from the Agricultural Surplus Production in Financing Important Items of Expenditure in Farms over the Size of 5.0 StA during the Period 1966-67—1971-72 (in Rupees)

A : *Domestic Household*

		(1)			(2)			(3)			(4)			(5)		
	Number of households	Marriages, Funerals			Housing			Court Cases			Education, Medical Attn.			Sub-total (1) to (4)		
		Total expenditure	Share of income from sale of farm products		Total expenditure	Share of income from sale of farm products		Total expenditure	Share of income from sale of farm products		Total expenditure	Share of income from sale of farm products		Total expenditure	Share of income from sale of farm products	
			Amt.	%		Amt.	%		Amt.	%		Amt.	%		Amt.	%
Village 1	06	12,965	6900	5.32	1876	856	45.6	850	—	—	575	145	25.2	16,266	7,901	48.6
Village 2	01	6,000	—	—	550	—	—	—	—	—	1,400	400	28.6	7,950	400	05.0
Village 3	10	49,300	500	01.0	4392	1,037	23.6	4,400	2,750	62.5	5,000	2,600	52.0	63,092	6,887	10.9
Total	17	68,265	7400	10.8	6818	1,893	27.8	5,250	2,750	52.4	6,975	3,145	45.1	87,308	15,188	17.4

B : *Farm Operations**

		(6)			(7)			(8)			(9)			(10)		
	Number of house-holds	Purchase of land			Purchase of Cattle			Farm Bldgs./Stalls**			Land Improvement, Irrigation			Sub-total (6) to (9)		
		Total expen-diture	Share of income from sale of farm products		Total expen-diture	Share of income from sale of farm products		Total expen-diture	Share of income from sale of farm products		Total expen-diture	Share of income from sale of farm products		Total expen-diture	Share of income from sale of farm products	
			Amt.	%		Amt.	%		Amt.	%		Amt.	%		Amt.	%
Village 1	06	2,628	350	13.3	1,745	445	25.5	1,876	856	45.6	2,740	640	23.4	8,989	2,291	25.5
Village 2	01	6,000	1,000	16.7	600	—	—	550	—	—	800	200	25.0	7,950	1,200	15.1
Village 3	10	2,900	900	31.9	6,090	1,500	24.6	4,393	1,038	23.6	12,100	2,650	21.9	25,483	6.088	23.9
Total	17	11,528	2,250	19.5	8,435	1,945	17.1	6,819	1,894	27.8	15,640	3,490	22.3	42,422	9,579	22 6

Summary

	Total expenditure (5) and (10)	Share of income from sale of farm products	
		Amt.	%
Village 1	25,255	10,192	40.4
Village 2	15,900	1,600	10.1
Village 3	88,575	12,975	14.6
Total	129,730	24,767	19.1

Remarks : *Excluding recurrent farm expenditure.

**Investigations on buildings for housing and farm buildings were conducted as one item and under the prevailing conditions in the case villages it was difficult to differentiate between these two types of buildings. Therefore, expenditure incurred in buildings are equally divided under domestic and farm expenditure.

Source : Own Surveys.

pattern of investment which eliminates potential productive capital and explains why the agricultural production in the case area has not increased to any significant level.

The possibility to earn high returns for capital invested in traditional moneylending as well as other indirect advantages discourages surplus farmers from investing in productive purposes. A basic distinction exists between the direct and indirect profits/advantages gained from moneylending. Interest earnings for the capital invested are the direct profits/advantages and these can be quantitatively determined. Indirect gains such as the creation of dependency relations like bonded labour cannot be easily assessed. If the moneylender is primarily interested in gaining indirect benefits, then a credit transaction does not end in itself but rather creates the prerequisites for benefits which are expected to be achieved afterwards.

Patnaik suggests that these indirect profits and advantages of traditional moneylending have contributed decisively to the increased investments of agricultural surplus in moneylending:

> High rates of surplus value were generated on the basis of destitute labour; but very rarely did this find its way back into agricultural investment, into capital intensification. The commonest avenues of surplus utilization remained the precapitalistic ones of moneylending, trade and purchase of land to let out to tenants. . . . The reason was simply the high rates of return available on the traditional avenues of investment, given a mass of pauperised peasants prepared to pay . . . usurious rates of interest on loan.[13]

Patnaik differentiates between the investment patterns of the 'Dominant Landholder' or the 'Rich Peasant' belonging to the colonial era on one hand, and the 'Capitalist Farmer' of the post-colonial period on the other hand. While the dominant landholder invests the agricultural surplus still in traditional applications (moneylending, trade, purchase of land), the capitalist farmer is oriented towards the expanding demand for agricultural production and invests more in productive ventures. It can be assumed, therefore, that an expanding market for agricultural products with parallel increases in income changes the investment pattern of farmers.

Since the conditions in the case area obviously are ideal for an increasing demand for agricultural production, the investment pattern of farmers should also have changed accordingly. Favourable marketing

13. U. Patnaik, "Capitalist Development in Agriculture, A Note" in *Economic and Political Weekly, Review of Agriculture*, Vol. VI, September 25, 1971, p. A-126.

avenues present in Dhanbad district should have inspired farmers to intensify their production by investing in productive purposes. In reality, however, the situation is different. This can be attributed mainly to the exceptionally high returns which can be earned from moneylending. Besides, there are no incentives for farmers to invest in development purposes. Surplus farmers hesitate to make rather risky investments to increase production but prefer the safe and certain way of making profits through moneylending. The investment pattern of surplus farmers is, therefore, almost similar to that of dominant landholders of the colonial era.

In view of the large number of deficit farms in the case area, a change in the investment behaviour of surplus farmers can be ruled out at present. The relations between surplus farmers (creditors) and small deficit farmers (debtors) in the case area are such that there exists hardly any possibility of transforming the traditional agriculture to achieve higher production outputs.

> The relation between big-farmer-moneylenders and small-farmer-borrowers can frustrate investment by both groups. The lender finds that further lending, to finance the dissaving of a growing population, offers higher returns than investment on his own land can do. The borrower does not use spare cash for farm investment opportunities (even when they offer a high expectation of return), because it is earmarked to pay off old and costly debts.[14]

Circle of Persons Engaged in Traditional Moneylending

The results from the observation of the traditional credit market lead us to the conclusion that the traditional village credit market is composed of a multitude of smaller, regionally restricted markets. The extent of these smaller markets at any given time is limited to the credit relations between parties located in the villages (Inner Circle) and to credit transactions involving parties in the immediate neighbourhood (Outer Circle).

An analysis of moneylenders belonging to the inner circle with regard to the ownership of land and occupations indicates that they are mostly farmers cultivating medium and large sized farms. Simultaneously this indicates that the actual potential for surplus production is present in larger farms and that a part of the surplus of these farms is invested in lending purposes.

14. M. Lipton, "Agricultural Finance and Rural Credit in Poor Countries" in *World Development*, Vol. 4, No. 7, 1976, pp. 546-47.

A further analysis of the social status of moneylenders belonging to the inner circle which includes the holding of public offices and honorary functions in addition to landownership and occupations shows that the moneylender belongs to an influential upper class of the community which controls the village trade and labour market as well as key positions in village administration and cooperatives.[15]

The fact that a small landowning rural upper class controls the key positions of village administration, money market and village cooperatives quickly leads us to the inference that a personal union exists between the office holders in the village cooperative and moneylenders. Thus, the grotesque situation arises that one and the same group of people guard over interests which pursue opposite objectives, since the cooperatives were primarily organised in order to curb the power of the moneylender. It is a paradoxical situation in which those people administer the institution which was created to eliminate them. Since a positive correlation exists between social status and ownership of land, it is consequently the castes with the highest social prestige which are active in moneylending. In the case villages it is the traditional Bhumihar or Brahmin caste of landlords, the merchant caste of Baniyas, and as an exception in Village 1, the dominating Kurmi Mahatos who control moneylending.

Moneylenders belonging to the outer circle are similar in the aspects mentioned above to those in the inner circle. They, too, are mostly large farmers living in villages in the neighbourhood of the villages under survey. It is interesting to note that most moneylenders belonging to the outer circle in Village 1 are called Maghaya by their clients. This indicates that the moneylenders in this village are former immigrants from Gaya and called after the historic Maghadha kingdom which had its centre in Gaya. The Maghayas are Hindus and Bihari landowners and belong to the Bhumihar caste.[16] In addition to Bhumihars, members of the Goala caste are also engaged in moneylending in the outer circle of Village 1. Moneylenders of the outer circle in Village 3 are Bhumihars and this demonstrates that traditional Bihari landowners play a predominant role in moneylending in the case area. Schwerin has pointed out that even at the time of the Second Settlement (1920-1935) it was almost exclusively the Biharis and Bengalis, i.e., Dikus, who conducted moneylending business in Chota Nagpur. The others mentioned were Baniyas

15. The social status is determined by caste, ownership of land, educational level, income, honorary functions and holding of key positions in the village administration.

16. E. Schmitt, "Die bevoelkerungsgeschichtliche Entwicklung. . .", op. cit., p. 43.

and especially the Babhans (Bhumihars). Actually, Dikus are an alien group of Hindus; they are not an autochthonous portion of the village population.[17]

MONEYLENDING IN VILLAGE 1

At first glance it is surprising to note the relatively large number of households appearing to be moneylenders in Village 1. However, analysing these moneylender-households in regard to the regularity, frequency and extent of their credit transactions, it can be observed that out of a total of 14 moneylenders in the inner circle and 18 in the outer circle, only four of each circle can actually be considered as moneylenders. These four households were active in their credit dealings throughout the period of this study. The others are so-called Amateur Moneylenders who engage occasionally in the lending business—depending on their financial position—and whose activities are limited to small loans.

Out of a total value of Rs. 56,468 granted as loans by traditional moneylenders both in cash and kind during the period of this study, loans to the value of Rs. 24,507 (43.4%) and Rs. 31,961 (56.6%) were given by moneylenders in the inner and outer circles respectively. The major part of these loans, amounting to a value of Rs. 49,501 (87.7%) originated from genuine moneylenders (see Table 1.3).

While a greater part of credit transactions in Villages 2 and 3 are in cash, loans in the form of kind are very common in Village 1 (amounting to 54.9% of all loans). This is mainly due to the chronic deficit in the supply situation of many households compelling them to borrow regularly from village moneylenders. Based on the number of households, there are 4.6 moneylender-loans per household, which clearly shows that some households approach the moneylender every year to get loans. Only nine households in Village 1 were not indebted to moneylenders.

MONEYLENDING IN VILLAGE 2

Village 2 is more centrally situated and far better accessible than the two other case villages. The occupation structure in Village 2 differs from Village 1 where agriculture is the main source of income. Many people in Village 2 are only subsistence farmers having small pieces of land. Due to the change in the occupation and income structure moneylending plays a relatively insignificant role in this village. Comparing

17. D. Schwerin, *Von Armut zu Elend.* Kolonialherrschaft und Agrarverfassung in Chota Nagpur, 1858-1908, Beitraege zur Suedasienforschung, Suedasien-Institut, Universitaet Heidelberg, Bd. 31, Wiesbaden, 1977, pp. 319, 496.

TABLE 1.3

Credit Transactions of Selected Moneylenders of Inner and Outer Circle in the Case Villages during the Period 1966/67—1971/72 (in Rupees)

Circle	No.	Moneylender	Item	Village (1)		Village (2)		Village (3)	
INNER CIRCLE	(1)	A_i	Amount	7,800		3,430		5,355	
			% of (6)		31.9		95.3		64.4
			% of (13)		13.8		71.7		23.2
	(2)	B_i	Amount	6,892		—		955	
			% of (6)		28.1		—		11.5
			% of (13)		12 2		—		4.1
	(3)	C_i	Amount	4,000		—		750	
			% of (6)		16.3		—		9.1
			% of (13)		7.1		—		3.3
	(4)	D_i	Amount	3,660		—		650	
			% of (6)		14.9		—		7.3
			% of (13)		6.5		—		2.8
	(5)	Misc.	Amount	2,155		170		600	
			% of (6)		8.8		4.7		7.2
			% of (13)		3.8		3.5		2.6
	(6)	Sub-Total (1) to (5)	Amount	24,507		3,600		8,310	
			% of (6)		100.0		100.0		100.0
			% of (13)		43.4		75.2		36.0
OUTER CIRCLE	(7)	A_o	Amount	8,048		—		9,300	
			% of (6)		25.2		—		62.9
			% of (13)		14.3		—		40.2
	(8)	B_o	Amount	7,516		—		3,600	
			% of (12)		23.5		—		24.3
			% of (13)		13.3		—		15.6
	(9)	C_o	Amount	6,155		—		—	
			% of (12)		19.3		—		—
			% of (13)		10.9		—		—
	(10)	D_o	Amount	3,430		—		—	
			% of (12)		17.0		—		—
			% of (13)		9.6		—		—
	(11)	Misc.	Amount	4,812		1,185		1,892	
			%of (12)		15.0		100.0		12.8
			% of (13)		8.5		24.8		8.2
	(12)	Sub-Total (7) to (11)	Amount	31,961		1,185		14,792	
			% of (12)		100.0		100.0		100.0
			% of (13)		56.6		24.8		64.0
	(13)	TOTAL	Amount	54,468		4,785		23,102	
			%		100		100		100

Remarks : Moneylenders of the 'inner' and 'outer' circle indicated in the Table as A_i, B_i . . . and A_o, B_o for different villages are not identical.

Source: Own Surveys.

traditional moneylender loans with the number of households, the amount of credits per household per year is only Rs. 26.60.[18] The Mukhiya is a classic example of the concentration of economic power and official functions in this village. Out of a total of 14 debtors, 12 obtained loans from the Mukhiya. The total value of loans given by the Mukhiya alone amounts to Rs. 3,430 or 95.3%. This represents 71.7% of all credit transactions handled by traditional moneylenders during the period of our survey. Most of these loans are in cash and only 15.3% are in kind.

Power and ownership patterns are extremely unilateral in Village 2, clearly illustrating that an unhindered control over the key areas of the village community—particularly the institutional and traditional credit markets—can be exploited to ensure a permanent and long term source of cheap labour. By means of his dominating position in the village cooperative the moneylender can prevent any party from having access to the cooperative. Thus, out of a total of 10 scheduled caste (Rajwar) households in this village, only two are members of the cooperative society. The majority of the villagers are, therefore, compelled to borrow from the Mukhiya, who is the only moneylender in this village.

MONEYLENDING IN VILLAGE 3

Both inner and outer circles of the traditional credit market in Village 3 are controlled by upper class households (Brahmins, Bhumihars). Moneylenders in the outer circle are more active and 64% of all credit dealings, amounting to a value of Rs. 14,792, were handled by them. This is mainly because the upper class households in the village obtain their loans mostly from moneylenders in adjacent villages who belong to their own castes. Although these upper class households have relatively large farms, they are compelled to obtain loans because of heavy expenses involved in family events such as marriages. They themselves cannot, therefore, engage in moneylending on a larger scale but with their limited resources they are able to handle the small credit needs of underprivileged castes in the village. The borrowers are not only debtors to these upper class households, but become also a potential labour force for them.

Based on the caste structure, the credit market in Village 3 can be subdivided into two sections: upper class households which obtain loans from moneylenders belonging to similar castes in the outer circle and the lower castes who borrow from lenders in the inner circle consisting of upper class households. Loans in kind are very few—amounting to only

18. The respective figures for Village 1 and Village 2 are Rs. 159.50 and Rs. 124.20.

Rs. 1,252 or 5.4%. These are given almost exclusively to subsistence farmers belonging to Scheduled castes. Upper class households usually borrow cash and 90% of such cash loans are underwritten by propert titles.[19]

Coverage and Forms of Traditional Credit Markets

The fragmentation of the informal credit system into a multitude of small credit markets of limited extent can be illustrated both from the viewpoint of the lender as of the borrower. On the part of the lender, we can principally suggest that the lender seeks as far as possible to preclude the risk of delinquency. One possibility for eliminating this risk, or holding it under control, is to restrict credit transactions to clients living in the local proximity and who can, therefore, be reached and confronted by the creditor at any time.

The upper class of the agrarian society to which the creditor usually belongs dominates the territory of these fragmented credit markets with a social and economic hegemony. The high social status of the lender provides him with a variety of possibilities to dictate and implement his terms of business, and, therefore, his claims. For instance, it has been ascertained that the moneylender:

> has different kinds and degrees to hold on those to whom he chooses to lend. . . . Usually, the compulsion which he depends upon is one which he has reason to hope will operate more or less automatically. If need be, of course, he is prepared to exert himself and set in motion the forces of compulsion. Those forces are social or economic or both. They are different for different debtors, but are in each case related to how the debtor is circumstanced in the village. The social compulsion is connected with considerations such as loss of 'face' or local prestige, caste disapproval, possible pressure through the caste-panchayat, and a variety of other social sanctions which, because they happen to be intangible, are not on that account any the less powerful. There are also a number of ways of economic compulsion. One form of pressure is that which the moneylender can himself exert by threatening to withhold further credit.[20]

From the above it should be clear that the moneylender's risk amounts to practically nothing.

19. See Section Mortgage of Land Titles as Security for Loans.

20. Reserve Bank of India, *All-India Rural Credit Survey*, Vol. II, The General Report, Bombay, 1954, pp. 171, 172.

The tendency of the creditor to use every possible opportunity to seize the land of the debtor additionally reinforces the spatial limitation of the credit activities and, with that, the creation of small credit markets. These ambitions of the creditor in the case area express themselves in a relatively high portion of credit arrangements which are underwritten by a legal title to the land.[21] Since the cultivation of the land is almost always transferred to the creditor himself, granting a loan underwritten by the property title can be transacted only when the land given as collateral is near the habitation of the creditor.

What holds for the seizure of the land of the debtor by the creditor is equally true for the labour of the debtor. The creditor's claim on the labour of the debtor and its use as a collateral for a loan is only guaranteed when the debtor lives in the region within the control of the creditor, that is, an area within which the social and economic jurisdiction of the creditor and their attendant control-mechanisms are in full sway. Moreover, since the borrowers are almost exclusively farmers, the same reasoning can also be applied to the creditor's attempt to expropriate the harvest of the debtor.

The reason cited above for the limitation of credit supply to local credit markets with restricted domain can also be given as reasons why a person can usually obtain a loan only in the circumference of his local credit market. This comprises the credit supply of his own village and of the villages in the immediate surroundings. In relation to this, Bottomly points out that:

> The cost to the borrower of going to a potentially competitive lending agent outside his district is likely to be considerable. The moneylender who does not know him will be suspicious until the farmer establishes a satisfactory repayment record. Initially, it is unlikely that he will be offered a competitive rate of interest, *if indeed he gets a loan at all.*[22]

Determination and Typification of Credit Market Form

The position of the village moneylender and the extent of his credit activities depend considerably on the presence of alternative credit sources, particularly institutional sources, and the availability of equal or more profitable avenues for investing surplus capital. Considering the

21. See Table 3.4.

22. A. Bottomly, "Monopoly Profit as a Determinant of Interest Rates in Underdeveloped Rural Areas" in *Oxford Economic Papers*, Vol. 16, No. 3, October 1964, pp. 432-33.

presence of institutional credit sources, the conditions in Villages 1 and 3 are ideal for maintaining the position of the moneylender without any interference. The activities of the credit cooperatives were restricted to short-term loan facilities as a unique interlude which merely substituted private consumption credits by institutional credits. Long-term effects such as creating a durable improvement in the incomes of debtors and reducing their indebtedness have not been achieved through institutional credit schemes in these villages. The only difference between Village 2 and Villages 1 and 3 is that Village 2 has a credit cooperative which can satisfy the credit demands of its members to a reasonable extent, although the loans are not primarily used for agricultural purposes.

On the basis of the morphological structure of the credit supply, local credit market form can be determined by the degree of market-domination by a supplier (moneylender) or a group of suppliers. Generally the market form relating to the supply typifies the competition between different suppliers.

The credit market deals with a homogeneous item (credit), irrespective of the credit type (cash or kind). Therefore, the degree of market-domination is determined to a large extent by the concentration of supply on a single, few or many supplier or suppliers. Although theoretically there are no restrictions to deter the entry of new traders in credit, and the market is in this respect open, the likelihood that new competitors will intrude in a village credit market is essentially restricted to so-called amateur moneylenders who cannot be taken seriously as competitors for the real moneylenders because their participation in the village credit market is marginal and limited in time. Thus, in a moderate length of time, it cannot be expected that the number of real moneylenders will increase.

The fact that traditional village credit markets are relatively closed and not susceptible to any potential competition is evidenced by the case of a newcomer who attempted to open a professional moneylending business in Village 1. Because of incessant threats and attacks by a group of local villagers he was compelled to close his lending business as quickly as he opened it. From the information of the villagers we may conjecture that the influential moneylender farmers pulled the strings for these measures. Apparently, the circle of established farmers-cum-moneylenders envisioned a threat to their monopoly over the village credit market in the activities of the newcomer. Later, a further example came to light; another outsider in the lending business was expelled, in the same way, from another village in the case area.

Bottomly argues that it is usually very difficult, if not impossible, for an outsider to break into an alien village credit market and maintain competition. This lends support to the inference that traditional credit markets are relatively closed. More particularly, Bottomly regards the activity of 'local social forces' predominating in the traditional credit markets as a chief cause for the low level of potential competition in these markets:

> It is very difficult for a potential competitor to break into a local market if he comes from another district. And this probably explains the frequent failure of governmentally inspired credit institutions to compete with local village moneylenders. Local social forces may even actively work against a competing lending institution.[23]

Table 1.3 demonstrates that the credit market in Village 1 is controlled by eight moneylenders, of whom four belong to the inner circle and the rest to the outer circle. With shares ranging from 6.5% to 14.3% they supplied 87.7% of credits given by moneylenders in the village during the period of the survey. The balance 12.3% is shared by the so-called amateur moneylenders. In relation to the total of 24 amateur moneylenders, this represents Rs. 48.40 per year, an insignificant amount compared to the credit activities of real moneylenders.

Credit supply in Village 2 is different from Village 1. While the credit market in Village 1 is almost equally shared by a group of moneylenders, the inner and outer circles of the credit market in Village 2 are dominated by a single moneylender. He belongs to the inner circle and has a share of over 70% of the credit business in this village.

Competition in the credit market of Village 3 is very similar to that of Village 1. Hence, too, the major share of credit activities (nearly 90%) is handled by one group of village moneylenders. However, the shares of individual moneylenders are different, ranging from 2.8% to 40.2%. In spite of their limited shares in the credit market, some of these moneylenders should be considered as real moneylenders because their activities are regular, although on a small scale. Most of these moneylenders belong to the upper castes.

The transformation of a market from an oligopol to a polypol form depends on whether there are few or many competitors. But the market form cannot be defined purely by the number of competitors, because the limit between 'few' and 'many' is vague. Therefore, the mobility and the limit of perceptibility of the demand must be taken into account.[24]

The types of active competition or the actual market forms can be defined as follows:

23. A. Bottomly, "Monopoly Profit as a Determinant. . . .", op. cit., pp. 432-35.
24. W. Krelle, *Preistheorie*, Tuebingen-Zuerich, 1961, pp. 47-48.

> A monopol market form exists if the demand on one supplier (monopolist) and another supplier or a group of suppliers is not perceivably mobile. In an oligopol market form there is a tangible mobility in the demand between one supplier and another or many suppliers, which is perceivable to all suppliers. The important difference between an oligopoly and monopoly competition is that in an oligopoly market the supplier cannot act alone in his decisions independently of other competitors. In a monopoly, the reactions of other suppliers in the same market are insignificant for the monopolist. A polypol form of competition exists if there is a tangible mobility of demand between the suppliers where the number of competitors is so large that any market-strategical measure of a single supplier will affect only him and not others.[25]

On the basis of the mobility of demand, the market form in the village credit markets can be characterised as follows:

> The credit market in Village 1 is almost equally shared by a group of moneylenders which indicates an oligopol market form. In Village 2, a monopoly exists in the credit market, since there is only one single moneylender. The situation in Village 3 is rather peculiar. Here, two moneylenders having comparatively large business shares in the credit transactions compete with a number of individual lenders having only smaller dealings. Because of the peculiarity in the nature of competition the credit market form in Village 3 can be termed as a form of partial oligopoly.

Due to the absence of credit cooperatives in Villages 1 and 3 during the time of this study there was no competition between traditional moneylenders and institutional credit agencies. In Village 2, however, which has a cooperative the situation was different since the cooperative could, at least theoretically, offer competition to the moneylenders. As mentioned earlier, Village 2 has only one moneylender and besides his monopoly over the credit market, he has also a dominating position in the village administration and cooperative. This enables him to prevent underprivileged villagers from obtaining membership of the credit cooperative and strengthens his monopoly further. The strategy of this moneylender is to subjugate underprivileged villagers to long-term debt liabilities in order to secure a permanent source of cheap labour. This objective is also achieved in Village 3 by undermining the efficacy of the credit cooperative through the domination of its key positions by the upper castes. Efforts of influential landlord farmers-cum-moneylenders to block access to the

25. W. Krelle. *Preistheorie*, op. cit., p. 43.

cooperative for underprivileged villagers and to obstruct the operations of the credit cooperative clearly demonstrates that the mere existence of an institutional credit source is considered to be a threat to their monopoly over the credit market by the traditional moneylenders.[26]

The Situation of the Demand

The demand for credit originates mostly from small farmers. These farmers have very little land and due to lack of any alternative earnings, their incomes are inadequate to meet daily needs. In the absence of any institutional credit agency most of these deficit households are compelled to borrow from traditional moneylenders. The terms of credit are often dictated by the lender.[27] Since the credit supply is concentrated within a restricted area and the prospective borrowers have a relatively good overview on the market, it can be presumed that they will, if they act rationally, try to obtain their loans from the most favourable source. This would, however, pre-suppose that the interest rates are different from source to source and that the borrowers are able and free to select the sources. In other words, there should be a tangible mobility of the demand.[28]

Mobility of Demand

If we submit the existing credit relations in the local credit markets between creditors and debtors to a deeper analysis, it will become very obvious that an individual party must usually obtain all his loans from the same moneylender. Consequently, the most prominent creditors have a relatively stable clientele of differing size which takes loans from the same moneylender throughout the period of this study. Considering the

26. In relation to this, Nisbet points out of the following : "At present the existing institutional lenders that service small farmers represent the only source of competition, albeit weak and limited, to the informal credit market. A small number of the rural poor currently has a choice of where to borrow. . . . Generally, the leadership or elites within the rural areas own the majority of wealth and income producing agents. For life to continue undisturbed the majority of the population must be kept poor . . . for the minority to maintain their grip on rural society." Ch. T. Nisbet, "Informal Lenders as Suppliers of Development Credits to Small Farmers in Developing Countries : Attractive or Deceptive Alternative" in *Small Farmer Credit, Informal Credit, A.I.D. Spring Review of Small Farmer Credit*, Vol. XV, No. SR 115, Washington, 1973, p. 11.

27. The bargaining power or negotiating position of a moneylender generally depends on his social status (caste, land ownership, education, etc.)

28. According to Krelle, the mobility of demand defines the fluidity of demand between two suppliers and, can, therefore, be used as a measurement for the intensity of competition. W. Krelle, *Preistheorie*, op. cit., p. 10.

mobility of demand, which measures the degree of competition between two or more competitors, this means that the mobility of demand is very low and, accordingly, very little competition exists in the credit markets.

The immobility of the credit demand is thus the result of a long-term business relation which can be of either voluntary or involuntary nature. Chandavarkar alludes to the same thing when he asserts that "farmers in the rural areas of underdeveloped economies are known to develop varying degrees of customary and traditional dependence on particular moneylenders."[29] Bottomly also sees in this one of the chief causes for the immobility of credit demand and expresses it as the "power of age-long custom."[30]

Voluntary agreements and business commitments are usually based on mutual trust between the creditor and the debtor. Hence there is no reason to make a change of creditor. Involuntary commitments, on the other hand, are crucial for the creation of traditional debt traps. Such involuntary ties are usually the sequel of debt liabilities which already exist and which drastically reduce the freedom of the debtor. It is quite possible that an initially voluntary agreement can turn into a personal liability which obliges the debtor to pay off his old debts and arrears of interest by manual labour on the farm of the creditor. Involuntary commitments in the form of personal debt and liability obligations make it impossible in two ways for the debtors to change creditors. Firstly, such an attempt by the debtor would incite the creditor to demand an immediate settlement of the whole debt, which most of the borrowers cannot afford even in the case of relatively small sums. Secondly, a person who is already indebted would have great difficulty in finding a new creditor who would be willing to grant credit to him even on barely acceptable terms. Besides, the creditor who is often also the employer has a number of other control mechanisms at his disposal (withdrawal of housing permit, expulsion from the village, physical violence, i.e., 'lathi strategy') which can intimidate the debtor into compliance. According to Bottomly, "local lenders may even resort to violence when a farmer does not pay. . . . Last, but far from least, among the factors reinforcing the private village moneylender's position is the element of social coercion".[31]

Moreover, a principle of professional courtesy between the influential moneylending landlords usually sees to it that delinquent debtors carrying personal liability cannot find a new employer-cum-creditor. Instead of an

29. A.G. Chandavarkar, "The Premium for Risk as a Determinant of Interest Rates in Underdeveloped Rural Areas" in *Quarterly Journal of Economics*, Vol. 79, No. 2, p. 324.

30. A. Bottomly, "Monopoly Profit as a Determinant, . . .", op. cit., p. 434.

31. A. Bottomly, Ibid., p. 435.

initially free choice of a creditor and employer a contractual compulsion sets in, and with the increasing duration of the debt, the credit receiving party is bound more tightly to the creditor and employer.[32] The fact that even the third generation of some of the debtors work on the fields of the creditor corroborates the point that involvement in a loan agreement almost thoroughly cancels the freedom of the debtor and thus the mobility of credit demand.

As mentioned earlier, the mobility of credit demand is also a measure of the degree of competition between the credit-givers. Therefore, we can conclude from the relative immobility of the credit demand that there is practically no competition between moneylenders of the same local credit market. This conclusion is as much as to say that a creditor from among the moneylenders who control the small village credit market has something like a monopoly; this makes it possible for him to trade on the credit without much regard for his competitors.

In summary, it can be stated that if the market form is determined purely on the basis of economic components relating to the market structure without considering the non-economic factors affecting the credit market, the prevailing conditions of competition in the credit markets will not be correctly interpreted. The theory of the presence of an oligopol form of competition cannot, therefore, be maintained since the economic components of an oligopol competition, to a large extent, are nullified by non-economic factors. The combined effect of the economic and non-economic factors has almost completely eliminated any competition in the local credit markets and this is one of the reasons that traditional forms of bondages still exist in the case area.[33]

From these findings we must infer, for at least a portion of the creditor-debtor relations, that the creditor seeks to obtain indirect gains besides the direct profits which come from the trade in credit. In this respect, the actual concession of credit is only a means to contrive an exploitation in the form of long-term debt and liability as they are couched

32. "The extra power given to a landlord-cum-moneylender in both land and credit markets can be enormous. Past, even inherited, obligations to particular lending families—aggravated by interest-on-interest—and by the need to make up in good years for defaults in bad years—can plunge poor, optionless groups into deepening 'spirals of debt'." M. Lipton, "Agricultural Finance and Rural Credit. . .", op. cit., p. 546.

33. Commenting on traditional forms of bondage increasingly prevailing in Bihar, Mundle states : "It is interesting to note that the phenomenon of bondage is relatively recent and growing. Of the sixty cases investigated only two persons were found who had been sevakias for 30 to 40 years. The large majority had fallen into bondage as recently as 10, seven or three years ago." S. Mundle, "The Bonded of Palamau" in *Economic and Political Weekly*, Vol. XI, No. 18, May 1976, p. 656.

in the terms of credit. The prevailing nature of competition in the village credit markets is ideally suited to promote such ambitions of the creditor. A similar conclusion is reached in a case study conducted in the Tundi Block of Dhanbad district:

> The creditors, however, do not always insist on full payment even in the long run. . . . They use this debt obligation to force upon the poor peasants an informal bondage and, therefore, a system of unequal exchanges thereby deriving enormous economic benefits such as cheap and assured labour . . . .[34]

34. P.H. Prasad, "Agrarian Unrest and Economic Change in Rural Bihar—Three Case Studies" in *Economic and Political Weekly*, Vol. X, No. 24, June 14, 1975, p. 931.

CHAPTER II

Interest Rates of Traditional Village Moneylender Credits

A common characteristic of traditional village moneylender credits is the relatively high interest rates irrespective of whether the loans are in cash or kind. The Bihar and Orissa Provincial Banking Enquiry Committee reported in 1930 that the interest rates of village moneylenders in Chota Nagpur area are considerably higher than those in the neighbouring areas.[1] After a period of more than twenty years, a survey conducted by the Reserve Bank of India in the districts of Hazaribagh and Palamau, close to Dhanbad district, again confirmed that the current interest rates of moneylenders in Chota Nagpur are "very high"[2] compared with overall Indian standards.

Interest Rates of Credit Markets: Findings of Own Surveys

In view of the different combinations of credit forms, involving both cash and kind and resulting in different repayment terms, it is necessary to distinguish between loans in cash and kind when analysing the interest rates of traditional village moneylenders.

The interest rate for loans in kind (usually paddy-loans) is charged as a percentage of the quantity of paddy given on loan. The quantity of paddy to be given as interest remains the same whether the loan is settled after one month or one year. Interest rates for cash loan are, however,

1. *The Bihar and Orissa Provincial Banking Enquiry Committee, 1929-1930*, Vol. 1, p. 33.

2. Reserve Bank of India, *All India Rural Credit Survey, Report of the Committee of Direction*, Vol. II, The General Report, Bombay, 1954, p. 190.

calculated on the effective duration of the credit. Interest is levied on a unit of currency (Rupee) and usually charged per month (Rupees/Paisas per month). In the case of paddy-loans, the quantity borrowed (capital) as well as the interest are settled only in paddy. Similarly, cash loans are repaid in cash. Thus, there are 'pure' cash loans and 'pure' loans in kind.

Another variation of credit combines both cash and kind. This is a mixed form and the interest rate, mutually agreed upon, is levied in the form of a specified quantity of paddy though the loan is given in cash. The quantity of paddy to be given as interest is determined per Rs. 100 and weighed in maunds, a measuring unit commonly used in the case area. Similar to pure loans in kind mentioned earlier, here too the interest remains the same irrespective of the credit duration. The capital sum borrowed in cash, however, has to be settled in cash, while the interest charges are in kind (paddy).

The system of interest calculation based on the effective period of repayment as practiced by institutional lending agencies, where the borrower has only to pay a pre-determined (nominal) interest rate is used by traditional moneylenders only in the case of pure cash loans. In all other credit forms, though the interest rate is pre-determined, it has to be paid without any relation to the repayment period. The moneylender makes no exception even if a farmer borrows a small quantity of paddy just before his harvest.

The majority of debtors are deficit farmers living on the verge of existence and, therefore, being faced with a recurring shortage of food just before harvest they are compelled to borrow paddy. The time of obtaining such paddy loans depends on the supply level of borrowers and varies between a few or many months before the harvest. Sometimes in extreme cases, paddy is borrowed just few days prior to the harvest. Traditionally, the interest for paddy-loans is settled soon after the harvest is brought in. Thus, the repayment period of pure loans in kind is determined, on one hand, by the degree of self-sufficiency (supply situation) of the debtor and, on the other, by the time interval until the harvest is completed.

The Effect of Seasonal Price Fluctuations on the Interest Rates of Moneylenders

The price of paddy is subject to seasonal fluctuations due to the shortage in the supply before the harvest and the abundance thereafter. The moneylender can exploit these price fluctuations to his benefit only if the loans are settled in paddy on the basis of the prevailing daily market price. Accordingly, the debtor has to settle the loan in paddy after the harvest at the prevailing low price but the quantity to be given in settlement has to correspond with the higher price of paddy which prevailed at the time of obtaining the loan. For instance, if a maund of paddy is borrowed before the harvest at a price of Rs. 20 per maund, the quantity to be given in settlement of the loan after the harvest corresponds to a cash value of Rs. 20. If the price of paddy after the harvest drops, for instance, to Rs. 16 per maund, the debtor has to give 1.25 maunds of paddy to the lender, which corresponds to a cash value of Rs. 20 at the prevailing price. Under these circumstances, the lender gains an additional profit of a quarter maund of paddy due to the price fluctuation.

If a debtor settles his loan promptly without being compelled to repay it through his own labour or if a loan is underwritten by a property title, then credit in kind is ideal for exploiting seasonal price fluctuations. But, where a loan is not settled on the basis of the current market price, as in the case of pure loans in kind, no additional profit besides the usual interest charges is gained because the quantity of paddy given in settlement of the loan is the same as the quantity borrowed before the harvest.

A quantity of paddy given as a loan before the harvest, when the price is high, has a lesser cash value at the time of settlement after the harvest. Therefore, if the quantity returned to the lender is equal to the quantity borrowed, the moneylender incurs actually a loss in terms of purchasing power. These losses are, however, compensated by the rapid turnover of capital and very high interest charges accrued within a short period. The capital invested in loans is quickly recovered to be reinvested in new loans. Further, the lender can store the paddy and sell it at a higher price at a subsequent time of shortage and heavy demand.

It can be also seen that a cash loan, if paid back in kind, brings in additional profits to the moneylender due to seasonal price changes. A loan of Rs. 100 given in cash before the harvest may correspond to 5 maunds of paddy, presuming a price of Rs. 20 per maund. If the price drops to Rs. 16 per maund after the harvest, the debtor has to give 6.25 maunds of paddy to the lender in order to settle the loan. Since the moneylender can make a clear profit of 1.5 maunds of paddy, he will obviously insist on a settlement in kind. If 3 maunds of paddy are given as interest for the loan of Rs. 100, the total profit made by the moneylender is 4.25 maunds of paddy. Thus, in terms of the quantity of paddy, the moneylender earns a profit of 85% in a period of about two months. In terms of the market price for paddy, the return is 68%. On this basis, the interest rate for a year could be well over 100%. If the same credit (Rs. 100) is given soon after the harvest, when the credit sum represents a paddy quantity of 6.25 maunds (at the rate of Rs. 16 per maund) and if the same interest rate of 3 maunds of paddy per Rs. 100 is charged, the net return to the lender both in the quantity of paddy as well as in terms of market price would be only 48%.

The credit period of such loans is inversely proportional to the difference in price and hence to the interest accrued. The reduction in the price difference due to an increased credit period gradually balances the interest return calculated on the basis of daily price with the net return expressed in the quantity of paddy.

The credit period of pure loans in kind varies from one year to a few days and cannot be exactly fixed. Therefore, interest rates for such loans cannot be calculated for a reference period of one year. In view of the fact that pure loans in kind are released and settled without any relation to price fluctuations, the interest rate for these loans represents, therefore, only a specific percentage of the paddy quantity given on loan. The fact that the effective interest rate is much higher for a shorter credit period than if calculated per year, is not taken into consideration.

The calculation of interest rates for mixed loans combining both cash and kind is similar. Here, too, the actual credit period is unknown and hence a clear relation between interest rate and credit period cannot be established. For instance, presuming a price of Rs. 20 per maund of paddy, the interest charged for such loans is 5 maunds of paddy per Rs 100 borrowed without any relation to the repayment period.

Interest Rates for Pure Loans in Kind

From the interest rates given in Table 2.1 it will be seen that there are two important rates for pure loans in kind. Out of a total of 218 such loans, 179 (82.1%) were at an interest rate of 50% while 33 (15.1%) were at 100% interest. The interest rate of 50% is typical for paddy-loans given for direct consumption. Loans in seed paddy carry an interest rate of 100% because this is more expensive than normal paddy. As loans in seed paddy are settled in low quality normal paddy, the high interest rate is meant to compensate for the loss in price. The interest rate of 75% is levied for loans given both in normal and seed paddy, where the percentage represents the arithmetical average of 50% and 100%. Most of the loans in kind (seed paddy and normal paddy), therefore, are given on uniform conditions. Any differences in credit terms are purely due to the quality of paddy given on loan corresponding to the purpose for which the paddy loan is taken. Factors such as the bargaining power and land ownership of the debtor, for instance, have no effect on the interest rates for loans in kind (see Table 2.2). The interest rates have not been modified even in times of shortages when unfavourable climatic conditions created crop failures as in 1966-67. This demonstrates clearly that the interest rates for paddy loans have been, more or less, institutionalised.

TABLE 2.1

Distribution of Interest Rates* Charged by Moneylenders of 'Inner' and 'Outer' Circle for Paddy-Loans Obtained during the Period 1966/67—1971-72**

	0%		25%		50%		75%		100%		Total	
	No.	%	No.	%	No.	%	No.	%	No.	%	No.	%
Village 1	—	—	—	—	158	82.3	03	01.6	31	16.1	192	100
Village 2	02	16.7	01	08.3	08	66.7	—	—	01	08.3	12	100
Village 3	—	—	—	—	13	92.9	—	—	01	07.1	14	100
Total	02	00.9	01	00.5	179	82.1	03	01.4	33	15.1	218	100

Remarks: *It has been already mentioned in the text that the interest rates given above are percentages of the credit-sum, which have to be paid irrespective of the duration of the credit (whether it is one, three or twelve month/s) after the harvest in form of kind.

**Inclusive of interest rates for credits given by the so-called 'Amateur Moneylenders'.

Source: Own Surveys.

TABLE 2.2

Distribution of Interest Rates* Charged by Moneylenders of 'Inner' and 'Outer' Circle for Paddy-Loans Obtained during the Period 1966/67—1971/72 Classified according to Farm Sizes**

Farm size class (StA)	0%		25%		50%		75%		100%		Total	
	No.	%	No.	%	No.	%	No.	%	No.	%	No.	%
Under 2.0	02	02.2	01	01.0	73	73.0	02	02.0	22	22.0	100	100
2.01— 5.0	—	—	—	—	87	89.7	01	01.0	09	09.3	97	100
5.01—10.0	—	—	—	—	19	90.5	—	—	02	09.5	21	100
Over 10.0	—	—	—	—	—	—	—	—	—	—	—	—
Total	02	00.9	01	00.5	179	82.1	03	01.4	33	15.1	218	100

Remarks: *It has been already mentioned in the text that the interest rates given above are percentages of the credit-sum, which have to be paid irrespective of the duration of the credit (whether it is one, three or twelve month/s) after the harvest in form of kind.

**Inclusive of interest rates for credits given by the so-called 'Amateur Moneylenders'.

Source: Own Surveys.

Interest Rates for Cash Loans

Interest rates for pure cash loans and for cash loans where interest is charged in kind are summarised in Table 2.3. The rates for pure cash loans are given on a p.a. (per annum) basis. Interest rates for mixed loans are based on a price of Rs. 20 per maund of paddy. Since the credit period of such loans is unknown, the interest cannot be calculated on an yearly rate. Assuming an average credit period of six months for mixed loans, the effective interest rate should, therefore, be estimated at exactly twice when calculated per year in order to make a direct comparison with the interest rates charged for pure cash loans. This is very important in order to assess the situation in the credit market correctly. Compared with the interest rates for pure loans in kind, the rates for cash loans are distributed over a wider range, varying from 0% to 300%. There are 14 different rates; Village 2 has the least number of rates—only 4. The number of rates is much higher in Villages 1 and 3 which have 10 and 11 different rates respectively. The wide variations are partly due to technical reasons as a result of summarising interest rates for different credit types to form a statistical overview. Another reason is the different gradings in interest charges based on monetary units whether Rs. 100 or Re. 1. For pure cash loans the rates are charged according to the decimal system of Paisa/Rupee and partly on the traditional system of Annas/Rupee. For mixed credits the rates are based on Maunds/Rupees 100.[3]

It is evident from Table 2.3 that interest rates prevailing in Village 2 (excluding mortgage loans) indicate that pure cash loans are common in this village. Many households in this village are engaged in trade and handicrafts and require cash for their work; their earnings are also in cash. Therefore, loan repayments (capital as well as interest) are mostly in cash.

3. The common interest rates charged for pure cash loans in the case villages are agreed upon as follows: 3 Paisa per Rupee per Month, 6 Paisa per Rupee per Month, 1 Anna per Rupee per Month, 10 Paisa per Rupee per Month, 2 Annas per Rupee per Month, 15 Paisa per Rupee per Month, 4 Annas per Rupee per Month. The corresponding percentages are 36, 60, 72, 75, 120, 150, 180 and 300% respectively. In the case of mixed credits, the interest rates are graded on the basis of the different quantities of paddy, which are fixed in maunds for a credit sum of Rs. 100. Here, rates such as 2.5 maunds per Rs. 100, 3 maunds per Rs. 100, 4 maunds per Rs. 100, and 5 maunds per Rs. 100 correspond with percentage interest rates of 50, 60, 80 and 100 given in Table 2.3. The fact that higher interest rates are charged when the time of obtaining the loan is closer to the harvest would explain the reason for the grading of interest rates. Thus, the different interest rates could be due to increasing shortages of paddy stocks. Should this presumption be correct, then a relation between the credit period and the amount of interest can be found also for mixed forms of credits.

In Villages 1 and 3 agriculture is still the main source of income. Here, most loans are given in cash but are settled in kind after the harvest.

While it was not possible to ascertain a common rate of interest for cash loans in these villages, it was found that rates between 50% and 100% are generally levied in villages where agriculture is dominant; rates below 50% are exceptional. In Village 2, however, the usual rates are below 50%. Rates over 100% are charged only in Village 1. On an yearly basis, the number of mixed loans carrying interest rates of over 100% are higher in agriculturally-oriented villages which indicates that interest rates exceeding 100% for cash loans are common in these villages. The actual rates charged can be much higher than those given in Table 2.3. Since the interest rates for pure loans in kind are not charged per annum, it can be also concluded that the majority of such loans in these villages also carry rates of interest exceeding 100%.

Interest Rates for Cash Loans according to Farm Sizes

The distribution of interest rates for cash loans according to farm size categories is shown in Table 2.4; out of a total of 131 cash loans, 116 or 88.5% were given to farms under the size of 5 Standard Acres. Further, it is seen that interest rates for cash loans are very different; they range from 0% to 300%.

A typical or common rate for farms below the size of 5 Standard Acres, however, cannot be determined although certain rates such as 72% and 100% are more frequent. Generally, it can be stated that rates below 50% are rarely charged from farms below the size of 5 Standard Acres; rates between 50% and 100% are, more or less, common. Farms over the size of 5 Standard Acres usually obtain mortgage loans. Out of a total of 15 cash loans given to farms in this category, 11 or 73.3% are against title mortgages. The rest are given on conditions similar to those applicable to smaller farms. Therefore, unlike pure loans in kind, there are no differences in interest rates according to farm sizes. The loans are usually on the same conditions, irrespective of the land ownership or social status of the debtor.

As mentioned earlier, the interest rates for pure cash loans varies between 0% to 300% even though the farms of debtors are of a similar size. The different rates cannot be attributed to objective factors alone such as the time interval between credit-release and harvest, a criteria determining the interest rate for mixed loans. It can be assumed here that the interest rates for pure cash loans are determined by a number of objective as well as subjective factors.

TABLE 2.3

Distribution of Interest Rates for Cash Loans of Moneylenders in the Inner and Outer Circle during 1966-67—1971/72**

		Village 1	Village 2	Village 3	Total
0% p.a.*	No.	—	02	01	03
	%	—	10.5	03.2	02.3
20% p.a.	No.	—	04	01	05
	%	—	21.1	03.2	03.8
36% p.a.	No.	05	—	01	06
	%	06.2	—	03.2	04.6
50% p.a.*	No.	09	—	01	10
	%	11.1	—	03.2	07.6
60% p.a.*	No.	02	—	02	04
	%	02.3	—	06.5	03.1
72% p.a.	No.	07	06	01	14
	%	08.6	31.6	03.2	10.7
75% p.a.	No.	03	—	—	03
	%	03.7	—	—	02.3
80% p.a.*	No.	08	—	01	09
	%	09.9	—	03.2	06.9
100% p.a.*	No.	08	—	04	12
	%	09.9	—	13.0	09.1
120% p.a.	No.	05	—	—	05
	%	06.2	—	—	03.8
150% p.a.	No.	02	—	01	03
	%	02.5	—	03.2	02.3
180% p.a.	No.	01	—	—	01
	%	01.2	—	—	00.8
300% p.a.	No.	05	02	01	08
	%	06.2	10.5	03.2	06.1
Mortgage Credits†	No.	26	05	17	48
	%	32.0	26.3	54.9	36.6
TOTAL	No.	81	19	31	131
	%	100	100	100	100

Remarks: *Interest Rates charged for Mixed Credits, where the rate is not based on a period of one year.

**Inclusive of Credits given by the so-called 'Amateur Moneylenders'.

†See Section VI, Interest Rates of Mortgage Loans, p. 73.

Source: Own Surveys.

TABLE 2.4

Distribution of Interest Rates for Cash Loans of Moneylenders in the Inner and Outer Circle during the Period 1966/67—1971/72 according to Farm Size Classes**

		FARM SIZE CLASS (StA)				TOTAL
		Under 2.0	2.01—5.0	5.01—10.0	Over 10.0	
0% p.a.*	No.	03	—	—	—	03
	%	04.6	—	—	—	02.3
20% p.a.	No.	02	03	—	—	05
	%	03.1	05.9	—	—	03.8
36% p.a.	No.	—	05	01	—	06
	%	—	09.8	07.1	—	04.6
50% p.a.*	No.	05	05	—	—	10
	%	07.7	09.8	—	—	07.6
60% p.a.*	No.	01	02	01	—	04
	%	01.5	03.9	07.1	—	03.1
72% p.a.	No.	11	03	—	—	14
	%	16.8	05.9	—	—	10.7
75% p.a.	No.	02	01	—	—	03
	%	03.1	02.0	—	—	02.3
80% p.a.*	No.	04	04	01	—	09
	%	06.2	07.8	07.1	—	06.9
100% p.a.*	No.	04	07	01	—	12
	%	06.2	13.7	07.1	—	09.1
120% p.a.	No.	04	01	—	—	05
	%	06.2	02.0	—	—	03.8
150% p.a.	No.	02	01	—	—	03
	%	03.1	02.0	—	—	02.3
180% p.a.	No.	01	—	—	—	01
	%	01.5	—	—	—	00.8
300% p.a.	No.	05	03	—	—	08
	%	07.7	05.9	—	—	06.1
Mortgage Credits†	No.	21	16	10	01	48
	%	32.3	31.3	71.6	100.0	36.6
TOTAL	No.	65	51	14	01	131
	%	100	100	100	100	100

Remarks: *Interest Rates charged for Mixed Credits, where the rate is not based on a period of one year.

**Inclusive of Credits given by the so-called 'Amateur Moneylenders'.

†See Section VI, Interest Rates of Mortgage Loans, p. 73.

Source: Own Surveys.

The Stability of Interest Rates at Traditional Credit Markets

Dhanbad district belongs to Chota Nagpur, both ecologically as well as ethnologically. Chota Nagpur is one of the main areas where tribal groups have settled. The history of the population in this area is characterised by an increasing alienation of tribal groups by immigrant Hindus and traders, an alienation which began in the 18th century. The tribal lands were gradually acquired by them through moneylending and trade and the tribals themselves have been held in dependence and in bonded labour through generations.[4]

The exploitation of the tribals and alienation of their land by the Hindus and traders reached its climax towards the second half of the 19th century, resulting in unrest and rebellion among the tribals. Thanks to various persons, particularly British civil servants and German missionaries who tackled the problem of exploitation, there is an almost up-to-date record on interest rates prevailing during the 19th and 20th centuries in the case area which makes it possible to compare these rates with those being charged today by moneylenders.

Cuthbert, a district official of the British civil service, reported as far back as in 1827 that interest rate for cash loans was 6.25% per month, amounting to 75% per year. According to his notes, loans given in the form of seed-grains carried an interest of 100% per annum irrespective of the credit period. His records also indicate that the system of charging interest in Annas per Rupee per month which is still widely used by moneylenders, was in practice at that time.[5] A memorandum prepared by 15 German missionaries in 1876 states that interest rates of 37.5%, 75% and 100% were usually charged for cash loans.[6] A series of village surveys conducted by the Bihar and Orissa Provincial Banking Enquiry Committee in Chota Nagpur confirmed that the above rates were charged even after a period of more than 50 years in 1929/30 :

> The ordinary rate (for paddy loans) is 50%, and 100% is usually charged for seed and here again the full rate is taken, even when payment is made promptly at the harvest. . . . The rates for cash loans are also distinctly higher. Nothing below 24% has been reported, 37.5% is common and 50 or even 75% is not unknown for ordinary transactions in the village.[7]

4. E. Schmitt, "Die bevoelkerungsgeschichtliche Entwicklung . . .", op. cit., p. 11.

5. *Journal of the Royal Asiatic Society of Great Britain and Ireland*, Vol. VIII, 1846, p. 412.

6. *Papers Relating to Chota Nagpur Agrarian Disputes*, Vol. I, 1890, 17. 5. 1876.

7. *The Bihar and Orissa Provincial Banking Enquiry Committee 1929-1930*, Vol. I, Patna, 1930, p. 291.

Findings of a village survey dating back to October 1929 indicate that even interest rates up to 300% were not uncommon: "Money loans, when urgently required . . . may bear interest of two or even four Annas per Rupee a month."[8] The survey further describes a type of loan which is very similar to the mixed form of credits identified during our own investigations:

> There is a special system called Charra by which for a loan of Rupees 5 the principal plus 5 Rats of paddy, worth Rupees 10, has to be paid back at harvest time.[9]

Moreover, Mukerjee and Darling have reported that the interest rate of 50% and 100% for loans in kind is charged not only in Chota Nagpur, but also in other areas.[10]

Recent surveys indicate that the interest rates prevailing in the traditional credit market, which were identified during our own surveys, are valid not only for the Chota Nagpur region and Dhanbad district, but also for other parts of Bihar and even in neighbouring West Bengal. On the basis of the relatively continuous and chronological descriptions of interest rates charged by moneylenders over a period of almost 150 years, it can be concluded that the credit forms and the interest rates as well as the terms upon which the rates are calculated, have remained practically unchanged to date. Thus, there has been no significant change in the conditions of the traditional village credit market since the beginning of the 19th century.

Factors Determining Interest Rates in the Traditional Credit Market

The description of interest rates in the village credit market demonstrates that these rates charged by traditional moneylenders are much higher than the rates levied by credit institutions. Further, the rates of moneylenders have remained practically static over a period of about 150 years. Though the institutional credit system, in the form of credit co-operatives, was started in India as early as the 1930s this has had no significant impact on the exorbitant interest rates of traditional lenders. Even legislative measures, such as the Moneylender's Act introduced in

8. Ibid., p. 2.
9. Ibid., p. 2.
10. M. Darling, *The Punjab Peasant in Prosperity and Debt*, 4th edn., Oxford University Press, 1947, p. 181. R. Mukerjee, *The Foundations of Indian Economics*, New York, O.J., pp. 266-67.

Bihar in 1938, were totally ineffective. Although the law prescribes a maximum interest rate of 12% for moneylender loans, the actual rates prevailing in the case area are exorbitant and illegal.[11] In this regard, the findings of the Agricultural Finance Subcommittee in 1945 are, therefore, still relevant:

> While it is true that the moneylender is the most important constituent of the agricultural credit machinery in the country, it is not possible to justify many of his practices and the charges he makes for his services. Very often these charges are out of all proportions to the risk involved in the business and constitute an exploitation of the helplessness, ignorance and the necessity of the borrower.[12]

According to Bottomly, there are four factors responsible for the high level of interest rates in traditional credit markets of developing countries. These are:

Opportunity Cost[13]
Administration Cost
Risk Cost
Monopoly Profit[14]

Although most authors agree upon these factors as determinants of interest rates, there is, however, difference in opinion concerning the effect of individual factors.[15] While Bottomly states that Administration

11. Government of Bihar, Law Department, *The Bihar Money-Lenders Act, 1938* (as modified up to the 24th May 1963), Patna, 1963, p. 14.

12. Reserve Bank of India, *Report of the Agricultural Finance Sub-Committee, 1945*, Bombay, 1965, p. 74.

13. The 'Opportunity Cost' per monetary unit is the cost incurred by the moneylender which indicates the extent of loss in actual or potential income per monetary unit, if he abstains from diverting his funds for alternative uses. These costs are less if moneylending earns higher returns than alternative uses.

14. A. Bottomly, "Reply" in *The Quarterly Journal of Economics*, Vol. 79, No. 2, May 1965, pp. 325-327.

15. A. Bottomly, "The Premium for Risk as a Determinant of Interest Rates in Underdeveloped Rural Areas" in *The Quarterly Journal of Economics*, Vol. 77, No. 4, November 1963, pp. 637-647.

—do—, "The Cost of Administering Private Loans in Underdeveloped Rural Areas" in T. Shukla (ed.), *Economics and Underdeveloped Agriculture*, Bombay, 1969, pp. 406-418.

—do—, "Monopoly Profit. . .", op. cit., pp. 431-437.

—do—, "Reply . . .," op. cit., pp. 325-327.

A.G. Chandavarkar. "The Premium for Risk. . .", op. cit., pp. 322-325.

Cost is the major determinant for the high level of interest, Chandavarkar argues that Monopoly Profits are more significant.[16] According to Singh, it is the Opportunity Cost which determines the interest rates and, finally, Long concludes that the high interest rates are the combined effect of all the four factors together with the chronic lack of capital which plagues the agricultural sector of most developing countries.[17] Since the importance of these factors is assessed in very differing ways, it is not really clear which factor is the dominating one.

THE EFFECT OF OPPORTUNITY COST

In view of the facts presented while discussing alternative uses of agricultural surplus and with regard to the importance of the factor Opportunity Cost per monetary unit as a determinant of the interest rates at traditional credit markets, it can be assumed that the opportunities for earning a relatively higher interest return for capital invested in moneylending are favourable in a traditional agriculture. This is so because such agriculture has a deficit and a surplus sector so that the dominant landholder estimates his Opportunity Cost relatively low. Therefore, the effect of this factor on the interest levels in traditional credit markets should not be overestimated, more so since the moneylender achieves also indirect benefits in addition to direct profits.

M. Long, "Interest Rates and the Structure of Agricultural Credit Markets" in *Oxford Economic Papers*, Vol. 20, No. 2, July 1968, pp. 275-288.

K. Singh, "Structural Analysis of Interest Rates on Consumption Loans in an Indian Village" in *Asian Economic Review*, Vol. 10, No. 4, August 1968, pp. 471-475.

16. "... administration charges, together with the premium for risk, are probably the major determinants of the high level of interest rates which obtain throughout the underdeveloped world."

A. Bottomly, "The Premium for Risk. . .", op. cit., p. 646.

"Thus, on the whole, it could be maintained that the residual element represented by monopoly profits in the determination of interest rates in rural areas of underdeveloped countries could well exceed the sum of the other components, namely, risk and liquidity premia and administration charges." A.G. Chandavarkar. "The Premium for Risk. . .", op. cit., p. 325.

17. "To sum up, the opportunity cost accounted for more than 50%, risk cost more than 25% and distribution cost about 15% of the interest." K. Singh, "Structural Analysis. . .", op. cit., p. 475.

"The inference of this study is that interest rates on agricultural loans ... are high, possibly because of some monopoly in the credit markets, but primarily because capital is scarce, because farm loans are costly to administer, because the uncertainties of agriculture result in considerable loss through default and because the demand for credit is seasonal." M. Long, "Interest Rates and the Structure. . .". op. cit., p. 287.

THE EFFECT OF ADMINISTRATION COST

> As long as individual farmers remain small operators with relatively petty needs, . . . they will go on borrowing in small amounts, each of which require time to negotiate and recover, and the Administration Costs on each Dollar which the moneylender loan will continue to be correspondingly high.[18]

Bottomly attempts to substantiate with the above conclusion that especially Administration Costs determine the high interest rates of moneylenders. His argument can be accepted only if it can be established that the working hours of the moneylender are also devoted to other engagements, besides the lending business. As mentioned earlier, the majority of moneylenders are large-scale farmers and they do not usually attend to the cultivation work themselves. At least during the period between sowing and harvest, when most of the small credit transactions take place, the lenders are not burdened with cultivation work and hence are relatively free. On the other hand, Bottomly has overestimated the effective time required for granting a loan in general and to negotiate a single transaction in particular. After all, traditional moneylenders have earned quite a good reputation for their efficiency because their loans are released quickly and without many complications.[19] It is, therefore, quite clear that the credit dealings of a moneylender do not divert his time from attending to other alternative engagements and the loan transactions do not require much time. The effect of Administration Cost, therefore, should not receive so much value as given to it by Bottomly. Besides, Chandavarkar has also stated clearly that credit activities of moneylenders are a 'family business' which can be handled by other family members without disturbing the daily working pattern of a moneylender's household.[20]

THE EFFECT OF RISK COST

According to Bottomly, Risk Cost is the factor secondary to the Administration Cost determining the level of interest rates.[21] Without

18. A. Bottomly, "The Cost of Administering. . .", op. cit., p. 413.
19. U. Kiermayr, "*Kredit im Entwicklungsprozess traditioneller Landwirtschaft in Westpakistan*", Saarbruecken, 1971, p. 122.
20. A.G. Chandavarkar, "The Premium for Risk. . .", op. cit., p. 324.
21. "It seems likely, however, that administration charges and risk will be the most important factors governing interest rate determination in the poorer parts of the world." A. Bottomly, "The Premium for Risk. . .", op. cit., p. 637.

contesting that statement we should remember that a large part of moneylender loans are against property mortgages; besides that the moneylender has several effective ways and means to fulfil his claims and demands. Therefore, the degree of risk is low which is also the opinion of Lipton:

> It is noteworthy that traditional lenders protect themselves against such causes of failure, for instance by advancing loans in kind, by expecting repayment in kind or labour-time, by charging higher interest or by matching the type of loan to the borrower (many traditional loans are 'consols' with interest paid forever and capital repaid never).[22]

Lipton's argument is acceptable, particularly because in contrast to other authors, Lipton does not restrict himself to the direct aims and benefit-expectations of moneylenders but also studies the advantages which the lenders expect to gain even after the loans are released. The low risk in credit business is finally a result of such indirect and subsequent benefits. However, the opinion of Lipton that the moneylender attempts to compensate for the risk by charging increased interest rates (which may support Bottomly's theory on the importance of Risk Cost) cannot be accepted. The high interest rates are primarily not intended to minimise the risk involved but meant to overcharge the debtor to create a prolonged debt-liability resulting in a personal dependency and liability commitment after the lapse of the time limit set by the moneylender. Hence, the high interest rates are mainly not intended to minimise the risk but rather to create the prerequisite conditions to gain indirect benefits from the credit business. The moneylender is not primarily interested in recovering the loan capital because a longer indebtedness brings in more interest returns and protracted liability commitments. Thus, the high interest rates are meant to achieve two aims simultaneously.

Finally, a survey conducted by the Reserve Bank of India, in which 344 moneylenders were interviewed, indicates that the lenders themselves consider the risk of delinquency to be very low: "Nearly two-thirds of these moneylenders said only 10% or less of the total amount was doubtful."[23]

22. M. Lipton, "Agricultural Finance and Rural Credit. . .", op. cit., p. 548.

23. Reserve Bank of India, *All India Rural Credit Survey, Report of the Committee of Direction*, Vol. 1, The Survey Report, Part 2 (Credit Agencies), Bombay, 1957, p. 475.

Based on these findings, as well as the results of our own surveys, it can be concluded that the factor of Risk Cost as a determinant of interest rates in traditional credit markets should be given less prominence, particularly than that given by Bottomly.

THE EFFECT OF MONOPOLY PROFIT

In contrast with Bottomly, Chandavarkar considers the factor of Monopoly Profit as one of the main determinants for high interest rates. He states that:

> the wide gap between risk and the actual interest charged is largely explained by the Monopoly Profits of moneylending, which attracts the social odium of usury in these countries.[24]

Chandavarkar's statement also contradicts the views of Long and Singh, both of who give the least importance to the factor of Monopoly Profit. Chandavarkar attributes his argument to the findings of the All India Rural Credit Survey which has demonstrated that most Indian villages have either a few or no moneylenders.[25] Chandavarkar concludes that there is practically no competition in traditional credit markets due to the small number of active moneylenders:

> The available evidence at least for India suggests that the 'density' of moneylenders . . . is very low and as such highly conducive to monopoly in the business.[26]

Numerous other activities and functions of moneylenders, according to Chandavarkar, further indicate the monopoly of moneylenders.

In addition to the above factors directly related to the personal position of the moneylender, Chandavarkar mentions also other points, further strengthening the monopoly status of the moneylender:

> Within the environment circumstanced by the fewness of moneylenders and the extent of their monopoly power arising from the combination of occupations, there is a whole complex of social and economic factors which together restrain competition among moneylenders. The lender-borrower nexus is strengthened by

24. A.G. Chandavarkar, "The Premium for Risk. . .", op. cit., p. 324.

25. Out of 600 villages selected and surveyed on a random basis, only 10.3% of villages had four or more active moneylenders. Reserve Bank of India, *All India Rural Credit Survey*, op. cit., p. 466.

26. A.G. Chandavarkar, "The Premium for Risk. . .", op. cit., p. 322.

tenancy agreements, trading and family relations, physical distance, ignorance, social pressures, and sometimes sheer inertia.[27]

This striking description of the credit market, especially in regard to traditional socio-economic forces, contradicts the argument of Bottomly that other moneylenders are also attracted by the monopoly profits.[28]

Chandavarkar's arguments can be supported by our own conclusions presented earlier in connection with the discussion of the market form related to the supply of credit. The lenders usually restrict their transactions to a locally limited circle of clients in order to minimise the risk of delinquency. The operations of a traditional moneylender are, therefore, limited to his own village and sometimes only to those in the neighbourhood. Within this restricted area, the financial and social position of the moneylender is fully effective and he is able to seize the land, labour and crops of the debtor if the need arises. The low mobility of the credit demand resulting in very little competition between moneylenders provides the moneylender with a monopoly over his own credit market. Considering the social and economic factors active in traditional credit markets, and in accordance with the comments of Chandavarkar, it can be concluded that the factor of monopoly profit must be given the highest importance in determining the effect on the interest rate levels.

THE EFFECT OF THE DEVELOPMENT STANDARD OF A REGION ON THE INTEREST LEVEL

A study conducted by the Reserve Bank of India further explains the relatively high interest levels in underdeveloped areas in general and in the case area in particular. After investigating a number of indicators such as the standard of banking system and rural credit cooperatives, including a classification of 75 selected districts in three categories (subsistence level, monetarised, commercialised), the study concludes that there is a close relation between the development standard of a region and the prevailing level of interest rates. With increasing monetarisation and commercialisation, resulting in an increasing standard of development, the interest rate levels in traditional credit markets tend to decrease. Out of the 75 districts covered by the study, two neighbouring districts

27. A.G. Chandavarkar, "The Premium for Risk. . .", op. cit., p. 324.

28. "Why has one monopolistic moneylender not moved into the territory of another attracted by local gains? Why has such a chain of events not eliminated, or at least greatly reduced, the element of usury in the rural rate?" A. Bottomly, "Reply. . .", op. cit., p. 327.

(Hazaribagh and Palamau) are classified as being on the subsistence level, and these belong to the group of districts having very high levels of interest rates.[29]

Bottomly, too, identifies a functional relationship between the standard of development of a region and the level of prevailing interest rates. He states that "the interest rates in a poor country will almost certainly be an inverse function of the overall productivity of its farmers."[30] This indicates that the effect of the factors discussed earlier on the level of interest rates should not be estimated without taking into consideration the standard of development of the relevant region.

Based on the inverse functional relationship between the interest rate levels and the standard of development, the relatively high interest rates indicate a correspondingly low standard of agricultural development in the case area.[31] It can be stated that the effect of the factors determining the interest levels is more active in a credit market of an underdeveloped traditional agriculture than in that of an agriculture with a higher standard of production. However, according to Bottomly, this conclusion applies only to the factors of Risk Cost and Administration Cost.[32] With regard to Risk Cost, Bottomly's argument cannot be accepted without comment, since the moneylender has many possibilities to minimise or prevent the risk of delinquency. Such possibilities exist mostly in a traditional power structure and hence are characteristics of a traditional rural society. Therefore, the factor of Risk Cost should be given relatively less importance in a traditional agricultural society. Rather it can be expected that the risk of delinquency would be greater with decreasing traditional behaviour such as, for instance, improved educational standards and better awareness among debtors of legal avenues open to them and the access of underprivileged groups to courts of law.

In contrast with the factor of Risk Cost, a clear inverse functional relationship exists between the factor of Monopoly Profit and the general standard of development. Competition between moneylenders operating in

29. Reserve Bank of India, *All India Rural Credit Survey*, op. cit., p. 192.

30. A. Bottomly, "The Premium for Risk. . .", op. cit., p. 646.

31. In spite of several important industries in the area under survey, the dualism existing between the agricultural and non-agricultural sectors has not been eliminated. Besides, modern and intensified agricultural production techniques have also not been practiced, despite the demand from non-agricultural sector for food.

32. "High risk premiums are apparently inseparable from low levels of production, and they can only be expected to decline as farmers are able to harvest and market a large surplus. Moreover, it can be shown that the same is true of administrative costs on making loans in underdeveloped rural areas." A. Bottomly, "The Premium for Risk. . .", op. cit., p. 646.

the same credit market is minimised or eliminated by factors based mostly on traditional behaviour patterns and power structures. These factors create a monopoly and provide almost ideal conditions in the credit market for charging high interest rates and achieving indirect profits from moneylending.[33] Therefore, the effect of Monopoly Profit on the interest level is more forceful in a traditional underdeveloped agriculture.

The account given here does not provide conclusive answers to various questions relating to the high level of interest rates in traditional credit markets. It does, however, demonstrate the most important factors determining the interest levels and their different degrees of influence. It was shown that economic factors can form a basis for explaining the high interest levels only if such factors are assessed also in the context of socio-economic factors operating in the credit markets. On the other hand, analysing the traditional credit market purely in terms of economic factors would disregard the fact that not only economic gains are achieved by moneylending. Traditional moneylending also provides indirect benefits to the lender by creating social dependencies between the creditor and the debtor, which in turn lead to further economic gains for the moneylender. The moneylender makes his profit not only directly by collecting the high interest charges but also by exploiting unpaid or underpaid labour. This explains why a large number of farm labourers in the case area are still in bonded labour. *The National Survey on the Incidence of Bonded Labour* concludes that 5% of farm workers in India are under bonded labour obligations. The survey states further:

> This illegal practice is nourished by extreme poverty and the social system prevailing in our rural areas. Most of the bonded labourers, and many more who are still not bonded have just no possessions of their own. The only source which they can fall upon is the moneylender and they have been bonded mostly in lieu of debts taken for domestic consumption.[34]

Long-term Stability of Interest Levels

The phenomenon of interest levels in the case area remaining relatively stable over a period of nearly 150 years can possibly be explained by the fact that the dualism existing between the agricultural and

33. The indirect profits and benefits should be also considered as part of the Monopoly Profits of the moneylender.

34. *National Survey on the Incidence of Bonded Labour*, Preliminary Report, New Delhi, 1979, p. VII.

non-agricultural sectors in this area has not been eliminated and that agriculture has not developed due to lack of interrelations between these two sectors. This is an important aspect in discussing the stability of interest levels, since the farming sector in the case area has not undergone any major development and, therefore, still bears almost all the characteristics of a traditional system.

The behaviour patterns of farmers, particularly the upper class of dominant farmers-cum-moneylenders are traditional. This had an impact also on the stability of interest levels in traditional credit markets. Schultz states that the environment of an agriculture marked with traditional behaviour patterns has the characteristic that "the state of preference and motive for holding and acquiring sources of income remains constant."[35] It can, therefore, be assumed that the traditional economic equilibrium in village credit markets has remained undisturbed by external influences and effects and the interest rates usually charged are the result of traditional behaviour patterns and values.

In this connection, it is useful to explore why moneylenders usually charge interest rates of 50% and 100% and often not any other rates. This could be possibly explained by the description of tenure forms practiced in Chota Nagpur during the 19th century presented by Schwerin.[36] The so-called 'Batai Tenure' was the most common form, where the tenant gets 50% of the harvest and the party, usually the landlord, providing the seeds is entitled to claim twice the value of seeds given. There may be historical connections between these tenure practices and interest rates of moneylenders. The opposite case is also possible, where the tenure systems developed from the credit conditions of moneylenders. Hence, a definite conclusion on the origin of these interest rates cannot be made.

Debt Management and Interest Collection by Traditional Moneylenders

The elucidation of competition in traditional village credit markets shows that the moneylender is unhampered in the protection of his interests because of his monopoly in the credit market. How he carries out his interests and objectives in concrete individual cases will now be exemplified by the mechanism of interest-farming as practiced by lenders in the case villages. The mechanism of debt-farming is a vital function of the traditional credit markets and shows how the moneylender manages debts.

Table 2.5 shows the mechanism whereby the moneylender siphons

35. Th. W. Schultz, *Transforming Traditional Agriculture*, New Haven, 1965, p. 29.

36. D. Schwerin, *Von Armut zu Elend*, op. cit., p. 165.

TABLE 2.5

Mechanism of Interest-Farming Practiced by Moneylenders in the Case Villages (1971-72)*

	(1)		(2)		(3)		(4)		(5)		(6)
Village/Farm size class (StA)	Current** production		Disposal of† labour		Off-Farm income		Traditional credit sources		Total interest payments to moneylenders 1971/72		Interest due for credits given in 1971/72
	Amt.	%	Amt.	%	Amt.	%	Amt.	%	Amt.	%	Amt.
Village 1											
Under 2.0	2,980	91.0	—	—	218	6.7	72	2.2	3,270	100	1,132
2.01— 5.0	4,437	90.3	—	—	476	9.7	—	—	4,913	100	1,878
5.01—10.0	1,270	100.0	—	—	—	—	—	—	1,270	100	660
Over 10.0	—	—	—	—	—	—	—	—	—	—	—
Total	8,687	91.9	—	—	694	7.3	72	0.8	9,453	100	3,670
Village 2											
Under 2.0	—	—	540	64.3	300	35.7	—	—	840	100	126
2.01— 5.0	—	—	—	—	—	—	—	—	—	—	—
5.01—10.0	—	—	—	—	—	—	—	—	—	—	—
Over 10.0	—	—	—	—	—	—	—	—	—	—	—
Total	—	—	540	64.3	300	35.7	—	—	840	100	126

	(1)		(2)		(3)		(4)		(5)		(6)
Village 3											
Under 2.0	10	1.6	630	98.4	—	—	—	—	640	100	228
2.01— 5.0	157	24.3	430	66.4	60	9.3	—	—	647	100	30
5.01—10.0	220	100.0	—	—	—	—	—	—	220	100	220
Over 10.0	—	—	—	—	—	—	—	—	—	—	—
Total	387	25.7	1,060	70.3	60	4.0	—	—	1,507	100	478
Full Total	9,074	76.9	1,600	13.6	1,054	8.9	72	0.6	11.800	100	4,274

Remarks: *Mortgage loans obtained from moneylenders in 1971-72 are not taken into account.

**See text.

†See text.

Source: Own Surveys.

interest from old debts and current loans. It is evident that this mechanism of debt-farming and the accompanying management of debts reveals considerable differences. Whereas 91.9% of the interest due in Village 1 is paid out of the current production of the farms, the debtors in Villages 2 and 3 pay off the interest by manual labour in the fields of the creditor. The figures in column 2 are based on the statements of debtors about the number of working days spent on the farm of their creditor without remuneration. Under the premise that an average daily wage is Rs. 2, according to the unanimous testimony of the debtors, the amount of interest paid off in the form of involuntary work in proportion to the total interest payments in 1971-72 is between 64.3% and 98.4% respectively. The daily wage of Rs. 2, it should be noted, is considerably below the prevailing daily wage of Rs. 3.40 on the open labour market as ascertained by Kropp.[37]

Debt-farming highlights the previous conclusion that giving credit is not exclusively a goal in itself, but is rather the means to a goal. That is, making a loan does not only bring the creditor its avowed benefit, but is also indispensable for setting up the conditions to win indirect gains which spiral out of the credit-process. These indirect gains amount to the capture of a long-term source of labour that is cheaper than is available under the conditions of the open labour market. We are dealing here with a calculated contrivance of personal liability from initially innocent loan agreements; the management of these agreements by the moneylenders aims at creating long-term interest-serfdom. Primarily, it is parties of the underprivileged castes who are trapped in this vicious circle of interest-serfdom, in some cases into the third generation.

This type of debt management in Villages 2 and 3 can only be understood in the context of the unequal distribution of land and its resultant village labour market. The labour market is characterised by a high demand for daily wage earners for the big farmers especially during the peak seasons. A guaranteed long-term source of farm workers is procured through moneylending, which is indispensable for the creation of such interest-serfdom. The management of debts, thus, exposes the strategy of the moneylender and is simultaneously the means by which the moneylender fulfils his strategy.

The management of debts in Villages 2 and 3 also reflects elements of the rural Hindu caste system which was introduced with the spread of Hindu socio-economic structures during the process of subinfeudation of the case area. According to Schmitt, relationships of subordination specific

37. E.W. Kropp, *Einfluss des Bergbaus auf die Beschaeftigungsstruktur in laendlichen Gemeinden*, Beitraege zur Suedasien-Forschung, Suedasien-Institut, Universitaet Heidelberg, Band 19, Wiesbaden, 1976, p. 101 and Table 31.

to each economic class are implicitly contained in this caste system.[38] There is accordingly a social system in these two villages in which, quite in contrast to Village 1, the Hindu social order with its characteristic features has persisted and carried over into the present day. In particular, now as before, it is the land cultivating Hindus and traders, that is, members of the non-autochthonous groups, such as the Bhumihars in Village 3 and the Baniya clan in Village 2 who have established themselves in the case area and subjugated the small farmers-cum-labour potential to themselves through debt, or in other words, brought them to interest-serfdom.[39] Even today interest-serfdom plays a role which must not be underestimated in the agriculture of the region, where the traditional strategies and practices continue unchanged.

38. E. Schmitt, "Die bevoelkerungsgeschichtliche Entwicklung. . .", op. cit., p. 10.

39. Ibid., p. 11.

CHAPTER III

Mortgage of Land Title as Security for Loans

For a village farmer land is the main asset that he can provide as a security to obtain a loan.[1] In addition to the high demand for land other factors too have increased the shortage of land in the case area.

Dhanbad district has one of the richest coal resources in India. Coal mining has rendered large tracts of land unfit for agriculture. For instance, only an average of about 220,000 Acres, 30.9% of the total land area of Dhanbad district were cultivated during the period from 1961-62 to 1969-70.[2]

The stagnation in farming lands along with a relatively high population-growth during the two decades from 1951 to 1961 and from 1961 to 1971 resulted in a decrease of agricultural land per capita from 0.24 Acres in 1951 to 0.19 Acres in 1961, and again to 0.15 in 1971.[3] Thus, the district of Dhanbad has the lowest agricultural land per capita in India.

Findings of our own surveys, as well as of other studies, show that farmers give highest priority to purchasing land. Investments in land are given this preference mainly because of economic and social motivations. While economic motivations are aimed mainly at improving the

1. In a comparatively poor country. . . where there is little movable property apart from cattle, implements, and seed, . . . land is not merely the best, but often the only security that can be pledged by a borrower. M. Darling, "*The Punjab Peasant. . .*", op. cit., pp. 175-176.

2. *Annual Season and Crop Report, 1969-70*, Directorate of Statistics and Evaluation, Government of Bihar.

3. Census 1971, Bihar, *District Census Handbook, Dhanbad District.*

production levels, social motives are primarily to gain prestige. Besides, land has unique features, such as a stable value and earning capacity, which set it apart from other investments.[4]

These characteristics of land are often also the preconditions for finalising a credit transaction. While the earning capacity represents the usefulness of land and procures a credit, the immovability and stability of value provide the security for the credit. Therefore, land combines both procuring and securing functions for a credit transaction unlike any other asset.[5]

Forms of Title Mortgages in the Case Area

Basically, there are two forms of title mortgages in the case area. These have remained almost unchanged since the middle of the 19th century.[6] The two forms, known in English law as 'usufructuary mortgage against interest' and 'usufructuary mortgage against principal and interest' are both 'mortgages with possession'. In the local language in the case area these are known as *sud bandhak* and *mayadi bandhak* respectively.[7] The main difference between these two basic forms lies in the mode of settling the mortgage. The *sud bandhak* form prescribes no time limit for settling the mortgage and the earnings achieved by the creditor from the possession of the mortgaged land cover the accrued interest. The debtor has to pay only the loan capital to redeem the mortgage. In the case of *mayadi bandhak* form, the earnings from the mortgaged land which the creditor receives, cover the interest as well as the loan capital. The mortgage is fully settled after a predetermined period, usually 7 years.[8]

4. E.W. Kropp, "Kapitalbildung landwirtschaftlicher Betriebe im Hinterland von Dhanbad", SFB 16, Dhanbad-Projekt, unveroeff. Manuskript, Heidelberg, 1972, p. 29.

5. U. Kiermayr, "Kredit im Entwicklungsprozess. . .", op. cit., p. 51.

6. D. Schwerin, *Von Armut zu Elend*, op. cit., p. 326.

7. Compared to 'Simple Mortgages' where the creditor is not entitled to use the land which is mortgaged to him, the system of 'Mortgage with Possession' allows the creditor to make full use of the property. Schwerin has pointed out that only 'Mortgages with Possession' are practiced in Chota Nagpur. He has mentioned two mortgage forms called 'zarpeshgi' and 'bhugut bandha', which are identical to the types 'sud bandhak' and 'mayadi bandhak' described by the author. Hence, only the descriptions, but not the provisions and forms of mortgages have changed since the middle of the 19th century in Chota Nagpur. D. Schwerin, "Von Armut zu Elend", op. cit., p. 326.

8. Although the Chota Nagpur Tenancy Act prescribes a maximum term of 5 years for *sud bandhak* mortgages, this has only a formal character. The act merely sets a deadline, during which the moneylender has to earn a 'reasonable' return for the loan. If the mortagage is not redeemed after the prescribed period, the mortgage will be extended on mutual agreement.

TABLE 3.1

Transfer of Property Titles in Village 1

Agricultural Land of Debtor (in StA)	Extent of Agricultural Land mortgaged to Creditor (in StA)	(%)	Credit sum realised (in Rs)	Credit sum per StA (in Rs)	Year of mortgage Contract	Form of Contract	Limit of Contract (Years)	Origin of Creditor	Caste connection: Debtor	Caste connection: Creditor	Local Description of Contract	Purpose of Credit
00.8	00.4	50.0	90.00	225.00	1966	Verbal	Unlimited*	Village	Sched. Caste	Sched. Caste[a]	*Sud Bandhak*	Marriage
00.8	0).4	50.0	90.00	225.00	1966	Verbal	Unlimited	Village	Sched. Caste	Scoed. Caste[a]	*Sud Bandhak*	Funeral
01.0	00.25	25.0	90.00	360,00	1966	Verbal	Unlimited	Village	Sched. Caste	Sched. Caste[a]	*Sud Bandhak*	Marriage
00.9	00.12	33.3	60.00	500.00	1971	Verbal	Unlimited	Village	Sched. Caste	Sched. Caste[a]	*Sud Bandhak*	Marriage
	00.18		50.00	278.00	1971	Verbal	Unlimited	Village	Sched. Caste	Sched. Caste[a]	*Sud Bandhak*	Family Expenses
02.7	00.2	07.4	130.00	650.00	1971	Verbal	Unlimited	Village	Sched. Caste	Sched. Caste	*Sud Bandhak*	Marriage
05.0	00.4	12.0	500.00	1,250.00	1966**	Verbal	Unlimited	Village	Backw. Caste	Backw. Caste[b]	*Sud Bandhak*	Funeral
	00.2		200.00	1,000.00	1966	Verbal	Unlimited	Village	Backw. Caste	Backw. Caste[b]	*Sud Bandhak*	Family Expenses
05.7	00.7	12.3	1,000.00	1,428.60	1966	Verbal	Unlimited	Next Village	Backw. Caste	Backw. Caste[c]	*Sud Bandhak*	Marriage
06.0	00.15	06.67	120.00	800.00	1966**	Verbal	Unlimited	Village	Backw. Caste	Backw. Caste	*Sud Bandhak*	Family Expenses
	00.25		200.00	800.00	1967	Verbal	Unlimited	Village	Backw. Caste	Backw. Caste	*Sud Bandhak*	Conversion of Coop. Credits
02.5	00.09	03.6	80.00	888.89	1969	Verbal	Unlimited	Next Village	Backw. Caste	Backw. Caste[c]	*Sud Bandhak*	Conversion of Coop. Credits
01.6	00.15	25.0	150.00	1,000.00	1967	Verbal	Unlimited	Village	Backw. Caste	Backw. Caste	*Sud Bandhak*	Conversion of Coop. Credits
	00.25		130.00	520.00	1971	Verbal	Unlimited	Village	Backw. Caste	Backw. Caste	*Sud Bandhak*	Funeral

04.5	00.33	07.3	400.00	1,212.12	1970	Verbal	Unlimited	Village	Backw. Caste	Backw. Caste[b]	*Sud Bandhak*	Marriage
08.5	00.125	01.47	100.00	800.00	1970	Verbal	Unlimited	Village	Backw. Caste	Backw. Caste[b]	*Sud Bandhak*	Purchase of Cattle
01.5	00.125	08.33	200.00	1,600.00	1971	Verbal	Unlimited	Village	Backw. Caste	Backw. Caste	*Sud Bandhak*	Marriage
02.5	00.25	10.0	400.00	1,600.00	1971	Verbal	Unlimited	Next Village	Backw. Caste	Backw. Caste[c]	*Sud Bandhak*	Marriage
04.25	00.25	05.9	600.00	2,400.00	1971	Verbal	Unlimited	Next Village	Backw. Caste	Backw. Caste[c]	*Sud Bandhak*	Purchase of Land
02.25	00.25	11.1	300.00	1,200.00	1971	Verbal	Unlimited	Next Village	Backw. Caste	Upper Caste	*Sud Bandhak*	Purchase of Cattle
00.66	00.33	100.0	300.00	909.10	1967	Verbal	Unlimited	Village	Upper Caste	Backw. Caste	*Sud Bandhak*	Conversion of Coop. Credits
	00.33		800.00	2,424.24	1971	Verbal	Unlimited	Next Village	Upper Caste	Backw. Caste[c]	*Sud Bandhak*	Funeral
02.1	00.25	23.8	300.00	1,200.00	1967	Verbal	Unlimited	Village	Upper Caste	Backw. Caste	*Sud Bandhak*	Conversion of Coop. Credits
	00.25		200.00	800.00	1970	Verbal	Unlimited	Village	Upper Caste	Backw. Caste	*Sud Bandhak*	Conversion of Money-lender Loan
03.5	00.375	10.7	1,200.00	3,200.00	1970	Verbal	Unlimited	Next Village	Upper Caste	Backw. Caste[c]	*Sud Bandhak*	Marriage
00.5	00.125	25.0	100.00	800.00	1966	Verbal	Unlimited	Next Village	Muslim	Muslim	*Sud Bandhak*	Funeral

Remarks: *Although the Law (Chota Nagpur Tenancy Act) has prescribed a maximum term of five years for *Sud Bandhak* Mortgages, this limit has only a formal character. Due to various modes of Contracts in the case area, the prescribed limit is exceeded to the disadvantage of the Debtor. As it was not possible to identify the duration of the *Sud Bandhak* Mortgage in individual cases, the contract limit is given as 'Unlimited' in the Table.

**Credits settled.

a, *b*, *c* Loans given by the same Creditor.

Source: Own Surveys.

TABLE 3.2

Transfer of Property Titles in Village 2

Agricultural Land of Debtor (in StA)	Extent of Agricultural Land mortgaged to Creditor (in StA)	Extent of Agricultural Land mortgaged to Creditor (%)	Credit sum realised (in Rs)	Credit sum per StA (in Rs)	Year of mortgage Contract	Form of Contract	Limit of Contract (Years)	Origin of Creditor	Caste connection: Debtor	Caste connection: Creditor	Local Description of Contract	Purpose of Credit
00.45	0.0675	28.3	60.00	888.89	1970	Verbal	7	Village	Sched. Caste	Baniya*	*Mayadi Bandhak*	Marriage
	0.06		60.00	1,000.00	1971	Verbal	Unlimited	Next Village	Sched. Caste	Muslim	*Sud Bandhak*	Marriage
01.0	0.05	05.0	60.00	1,200.00	1971	Verbal	Unlimited	Village	Backw.Caste	Backw.Caste	*Sud Bandhak*	Medical Expenses
00.48	0.24	50.0	250.00	1,041.67	1966	Verbal	7	Village	Backw.Caste	Banyia*	*Kaila Bandhak*	Marriage
02.6	0.78	30.0	1,000.00**	1,282.00	1966	Verbal	7	Village	Backw.Caste	Baniya*	*Kaila Bandhak*	Marriage

Remarks: *This Creditor is the Mukhiya of Village 2.
**Credits settled.

Source: Own Surveys.

TABLE 3.3

Transfer of Property Titles in Village 3

Aricul-tural Land of Debtor (in StA)	Extent of Agri-cultural Land mortgaged to Creditor (in StA)	(%)	Credit sum realised (in Rs)	Credit sum per StA (in Rs)	Year of mort-gage Contract	Form of Con-tract	Limit of Con-tract (Years)	Origin of Creditor	Caste connection: Debtor	Caste connection: Creditor	Local Description of Contract	Purpose of Credit
02.2	0.24	12.0	200.00	833.33	1966	Verbal	Unlimited	Village	Sched.Caste	Sched.Tribes	*Sud Bandhak*	Funeral
0.55	0.11	20.0	100.00	909.09	1967	Verbal	Unlimited	Village	Sched.Caste	Sched.Caste	*Sud Bandhak*	Marriage
01.4	0.7	50.0	300.00	428.57	1968	Verbal	Unlimited	Village	Sched.Caste	Backw. Caste	*Sud Bandhak*	Marriage
02.2	0.55	25.0	400.00	727.27	1969	Verbal	Unlimited	Village	Sched.Tribes	Upper Caste[a]	*Sud Bandhak*	Marriage
02.0	0 2	10.0	200.00	1,000.00	1971	Verbal	7	Next Village	Sched.Tribes	Upper Caste[b]	*Mayadi Bandhak*	Funeral
05.0	0.25	5.0	300 00	1,200.00	1966	Verbal	Unlimited	Village	Sched.Tribes	Upper Caste[a]	*Sud Bandhak*	Marriage
00.83	0.12	43.4	100.00	833.13	1967	Verbal	Unlimited	Village	Sched.Caste	Upper Caste	*Sud Bandhak*	Conversion of Moneylender Loan
	0.24		300.00	1,250.00	1971	Verbal	7	Next Village	Sched.Caste	Upper Caste[b]	*Mayadi Bandhak*	Funeral
02.25	0.15	06.67	250.00	1,666.00	1971	Regtd.	7	Village	Sched.Caste	Upper Caste	*Mayadi Bandhak*	Conversion of Moneylender Loan
04.0	0.5	12.5	1,000.00	2,000.00	1966	Verbal	Unlimited	Village	Upper Caste	Upper Caste[a]	*Sud Bandhak*	Marriage
07.5	2.75	36.67	5,500.00[c]	2,000.00	1971	Regtd.	7	Next Village	Upper Caste	Upper Caste[b]	*Mayadi Bandhak*	Marriage
09.0	0.75	8.33	1,500.00	2,000.00	1971	Regtd.	7	Village	Upper Caste	Upper Caste[a]	*Mayadi Bandhak*	Marriage
09.1	0.7	15.4	1,000.00	1,428.60	1966	Regtd.	7	Next Village	Upper Caste	Upper Caste[b]	*Mayadi Bandhak*	Marriage
	0.7		1,000.00	1,428.60	1968	Regtd.	7	Next Village	Upper Caste	Upper Caste[b]	*Mayadi Bandhak*	Conversion of Moneylender Loan

(*Contd.*)

(*Contd.*)

09.46	1.18	20.0	2,700.00	2,288.13	1969	Regtd.	7	Next Village	Upper Caste	Upper Caste	*Mayadi Bandhak*	Marriage
	0.71		900.00	1,267.60	1969	Regtd.	7	Next Village	Upper Caste	Upper Caste	*Mayadi Bandhak*	Purchase of Cattle
12.0	1.5	12.5	2,800.00[d]	1,866.66	1966	Regtd.	7	Next Village	Upper Caste	Upper Caste	*Mayadi Bandhak*	Marriage

Remarks : a) and b) Loans given by the same Creditor.

c) This Loan has been advanced by two Creditors.

d) This is a Loan obtained from a relative, which has been meanwhile settled.

Source: Own Surveys.

TABLE 3.4

Share of Mortgage Credits in the Overall Credit Activities of Traditional Moneylenders and Share of Mortgage Credit in the Overall Debt Commitments to Traditional Moneylenders (in Rupees)

	(1)	(2)	(3)	(4)	(5)	(6)	(7)	(8)
	Credits underwritten by Property Titles	Traditional Moneylender Credits	(1) as a Percentage of (2)	Traditional Moneylender Credits for Marriages and Funerals	Mortgage Credits out of (4)	(5) as a Percentage of (4)	Debts to traditional Moneylenders	(1) as a Percentage of (7)
Village 1	7,790	56,468	13.8	26,840	5,190	19.3	26,123	29.8
Village 2	1,430	4,785	29.9	2,560	1,310	51.2	1,529	93.5
Village 3	18,550	23,102	80.3	19,050	16,300	85.6	18,880	98.3
Total	27,770	84,355	32.9	48,450	22,800	47.1	46,532	59.7

Source: Own Surveys.

TABLE 3.5

Mortgage Credits of Traditional Moneylenders according to Purposes of Use (in Rupees)

	(1)		(2)		(3)		(4)		(5)		(6)		(7)		(8)		(9)	
	Marriages Funerals		Conversion of Coopera-tive Credits		Conversion of Money-lender Credits		Household Mainte-nance Expenses		Medical Attention		Housing		Purchase of Land		Livestock Pur-chase		Total	
	Amt.	%	Amt.	%	Amt.	%	Amt.	%	Amt.	%	Amt	%	Amt.	%	Amt.	%	Amt.	%
Village 1	5,190	66.6	1,030	13.2	200	02.6	370	04.8	—	—	—	—	600	7.7	400	5.1	7,790	100
Village 2	1,310	91.6	—	—	—	—	—	—	60	4.2	60	4.2	—	—	—	—	1,430	100
Village 3	16,300	87.9	—	—	1,350	07.3	—	—	—	—	—	—	—	—	900	4.8	18,550	100
Total	22,800	82.1	1,030	03.7	1,550	05.6	370	01.3	60	0.2	60	0.2	600	2.2	1,300	4.7	27,770	100

Source : Own Surveys.

A third form of title mortgage similar to the *sud bandhak* form prescribes that if the mortgage is not redeemed within a specified period, the land will become the legal property of the creditor.[9]

Structure and Extent of Traditional Forms of Mortgages

As mentioned earlier, domestic events often compel the farmers to borrow from moneylenders. Tables 3.1 to 3.3 give the main reasons for borrowing and it can be seen that marriages and funerals are the main reasons; 31 out of 48 loans were obtained to cover the expenses of these events. Very few loans are obtained for productive purposes.

Table 3.4 gives the number of moneylender loans secured by title mortgages and demonstrates the importance of such loans within the framework of the traditional credit market. It shows that in Villages 1, 2 and 3 the percentages of loans underwritten by title mortgages are 13.8, 29.9 and 80.3 respectively. Village 3 has a high percentage of mortgage loans mainly due to the very heavy credit needs of the upper castes (Brahmins, Bhumihars) to finance the expenses involved in marriages, where the bride's father has to find a large dowry. Table 3.4 also indicates the proportion between mortgage loans and the total credit transactions of moneylenders and shows that most of the mortgages are for obtaining loans to finance domestic purposes. Except loans obtained for settling co-operative and moneylender loans (15.8%) in Village 1, other purposes are insignificant.

FORMS OF TITLE MORTGAGES IN THE CONTEXT OF SPECIFIC DIFFERENCES IN VILLAGES

Although the case area has a small range and the case villages are relatively close to each other, there are different modes of usufructuary mortgages practiced by moneylenders. Village 1 still has all the features of a traditional agriculture and the *sud bandhak* form is common. In Villages 2 and 3, however, most of the credit transactions between members of upper castes are based on *mayadi bandhak* form of mortgages (see Table 3.3). These mortgages are legally registered and have a limited validity period. But most of the mortgages between backward castes, scheduled castes and tribes, as well as between these underprivileged groups and upper castes are not registered and have no time limit. These mortgages have to be, therefore, classified under the *sud bandhak* form.

9. According to English law, this is known as 'Usufructuary Mortgage by Conditional Sale'. In Hindi, it is called *shart vikraya bandhak* and in the case area known as *kaila bandhak* or *kewala*, which may be due to language differences.

In Village 2, all forms of title mortgages are practiced.

The fact that only the *sud bandhak* form of mortgage is practiced in Village 1 can be attributed to traditional reasons. This form of mortgage seems to be favourable to the moneylender and, at least to some extent, to the borrower. The borrower can redeem the mortgage after a period of usually 5 years or, in the event of his inability to do so, can get an extension of the credit period in concurrence with the moneylender. On the other hand, the moneylender has the possibility to use the land for a longer term under the conditions of the *sud bandhak* mortgage if the borrower fails to redeem the land within the prescribed period. If the primary motive of the moneylender is to possess the land, this type of mortgage enables him to compel the borrower to sell the land far below the actual market value. Besides the genuine purchase of land, this is the only other way through which a moneylender can procure additional land. This should be one of the reasons which has inspired small and medium scale farmers in Village 1 to invest in such mortgages. For similar reasons, the *sud bandhak* form is also practiced in Villages 2 and 3.

As mentioned earlier, the *mayadi bandhak* form is common in Village 3. Credit transactions between upper castes are underwritten by this type of title mortgages. The selection of this form and the legal registration of mortgage documents are due to better knowledge and awareness of the borrowers concerning the legal aspects of these transactions.

Strategy of the Moneylender and the Negotiating Position of the Borrower

On the basis of our own surveys, it is not possible to make a general statement about the upper limit beyond which a moneylender will insist on a title mortgage as security for a loan. Basically, the moneylender decides on this question himself, depending on the assets of the borrower after taking into consideration the extent of lands owned by the borrower. The moneylender may not insist on a mortgage if the borrower has other established source of income besides land. In this connection, however, the motive of the moneylender is of paramount importance. If the moneylender aims at acquiring more land in addition to pure financial considerations such as interest returns, the lender will obviously attempt to obtain a mortgage even for a relatively small loan. This applies also if the lender is interested in imposing a liability commitment on the borrower which would subsequently result in bonded labour.

The amount of loan obtainable per acre of land depends on the fertility of the soil. As mentioned earlier, differences in soil fertilities can be eliminated to a considerable extent by converting all land areas to Standard Acres. However, the data still show that the fluctuations in credit sums obtainable per acre of land are relatively large. While the credit sums per Standard Acre of land in Village 2 are within reasonable limits, the variations are very marked in Villages 1 and 3; they range from Rs. 225 to Rs. 3,200 and from Rs. 248 to Rs. 2,288 per Standard Acre respectively. In both villages, these differences were associated with castes. It is found that the credit sum per Standard Acre fixed by moneylenders for transactions with scheduled castes is Rs. 373 while that for the backward/upper castes is Rs. 1,212 (almost four times more). The situation in Village 3 is similar, where the credit sums per Standard Acre for the above two groups are Rs. 983 and Rs. 1,785 respectively (see Tables 3.1-3.3).

It is quite clear from the above analysis that the caste-status of the borrower is the main factor which determines the credit sum obtainable per Standard Acre of land. A person belonging to a higher caste and, therefore, having a higher social status is in a better position to negotiate a larger credit sum than a borrower belonging to an underprivileged caste. It can be, therefore, concluded that the credit sum obtainable per Standard Acre depends finally on the bargaining power of the borrower rather than on other considerations such as the location of the land, access, etc. However, other factors like land ownership, educational standard, occupation of the borrower as well as his personal relations with the moneylender, too, may have an effect on the credit sum. The strategy of the moneylender, too, has a decisive influence on the credit sum. If the motive of the moneylender is to use the land for a longer period with a view to seize it later, the creditor will then deliberately grant a higher credit sum per Standard Acre. The borrower is thereby overburdened, creating a prolonged debt liability and the land may not be redeemed at all. In this context, granting a higher credit sum is not meant to earn larger interest returns but to achieve the indirect benefits mentioned above. A closer study reveals that the motive of the moneylenders behind the mortgages in Village 1 is to use the land given as security. In Villages 2 and 3, however, it can be presumed that the creditors are interested in creating bonded labour relations through the mortgage loan transactions.

Socio-Economic Effects of Traditional Title Mortgages

In economic terms, a title mortgage is a temporary disinvestment for the borrowing party. It is purely an intersectoral transfer of land with a temporary change in the ownership. The effects on the debtor and his income depends on the form of usufructuary mortgage. It is clear that redemption of a *sud bandhak* form of mortgage is more difficult as it prevents him from using the land during the credit period which can be very long. Usually the loans are obtained for consumption and have no positive effect on the debtor's income. His income actually becomes less because of the loss of his land. Table 3.6 demonstrates that the area

TABLE 3.6

Reduction in Farm Land Areas due to Title Mortgages in Terms of Overall Farm Land Area (in StA)

Fram size class	Village 1				Village 2				Village 3				Total			
	Number of households	Farm land area	Land area mortgaged		Number of households	Farm land area	Land area mortgaged		Number of households	Farm land area	Land area mortgaged		Number of households	Farm land area	Land area mortgaged	
			Qty.	%			Qty.	%			Qty.	%			Qty.	%
Under 2.0	08	30.8	2.660	8.6	03	19.4	0.4175	2.2	05	8.3	1.61	19.4	16	58.5	4.6875	8.0
2.01— 5.0	09	89.6	2.845	3.2	01	07.9	0.78	9.9	04	36.9	1.45	3.9	14	134.4	5.0750	3.8
5.01—10.0	03	34.0	1.225	3.6	—	—	—	—	04	56.9	6.79	11.9	07	90.9	8.0150	8.8
Over 10.0	—	10.3	—	—	—	18.2	—	—	01	35.7	1.5	4.2	01	64.2	1.5000	2.3
Total	20	164.7	6.730	4.1	04	45.5	1.1975	2.6	14	137.8	11 35	8.2	38	348.0	19.2775	5.5

Source: Own Surveys.

cultivated, particularly in some farms below 2 Standard Acres in Villages 1 and 3 has been drastically reduced which can be attributed to the loss of land due to mortgages.

Farmers having other sources of income are able to compensate for the loss of earnings due to mortgages. However, borrowers who have no such additional incomes will inevitably lose their mortgaged lands since very often they are unable to settle the loans when the moneylender demands payment. In case a debtor fails to settle a mortgage loan, it is conceivable that a creditor may abandon his idea of seizing the land and instead exploit the situation more cunningly to ensure a cheap supply of labour. A pure loan commitment would then develop into a personal dependency relation, obliging the debtor to work for the creditor probably throughout the lifetime of the borrower. Since the majority of the debtors are on the verge of subsistence, the effects of the mortgages are devastating.

In this context, it can be concluded that the *sud bandhak* form of mortgages is particularly disadvantageous to the borrower. It creates an uncontrolled transfer process of land increasing the inequality of land distribution, particularly in backward areas (as pointed out by Schwerin), where most mortgages are not redeemed due to lack of additional incomes.[10] Although it would be necessary to conduct studies over a longer period to make definite conclusions on the extent of land redistribution resulting from mortgages, it can be assumed, following the comments of Schwerin, that a large number of mortgages are seldom redeemed by the borrowers.[11]

Legal Aspects of Land Mortgages

The Chota Nagpur Tenancy Act prescribes the legal requirements and conditions relating to all forms of title mortgages in the case area. It has provisions to protect the land ownership rights of the tribal population and prohibits land mortgages by scheduled tribes to other castes unless certain conditions are fulfilled.[12] For instance, the act permits usufructuary mortgages (also for the tribals) with a validity period of not more than 5 years. In addition, it also has provision for a title mortgage form called *Bhugut Bandha* with a validity period of 7 years.[13] This is an

10. D. Schwerin, *Von Armut zu Elend*, op. cit., p. 338.

11. "In practice, of course, the creditor took permanent possession of the land, and this was probably meant from the very beginning." D. Schwerin, Preliminary Draft, Dhanbad-Gesamtbericht unpublished Manuscript, New York, 1976, p. 10.

12. *The Chota Nagpur Tenancy Act, 1908, As Modified up to the 15th November 1965*, Government of Bihar, Law Department, Patna, 1966, p. 35.

13. Ibid., p. 2.

usufructuary mortgage against principal and interest and similar to the *mayadi bandhak* form mentioned earlier.

In spite of the protective provisions in this act, a large number of mortgages in the case villages are not in accordance with these requirements. In Village 1 alone, there were nine such unlawful cases of mortgages where the prescribed validity period of 5 years for *sud bandhak* mortgages had not been observed.

We have already referred to caste-related peculiarities in Village 3 (see Table 3.3). While all title mortgages in this village with the exception of one case between upper castes are in the *mayadi bandhak* form and the documents are legally registered (similar to the *bhugut bandha* form in the act), most land mortgages between backward caste debtors and upper class creditors are in the *sud bandhak* form. Even here, there are five mortgages where the prescribed validity period of 5 years has been exceeded.

Vide paragraph 59 of the Transfer of Property Act any loan transaction exceeding a sum of Rs 100 should be on a written agreement and verbal dealings are, therefore, invalid.[14] On the other hand, the debtor can claim his property only if his ownership rights can be legally established. The borrowers are, hence, in a precarious position because most of them have no legal means to prove their ownership rights while a large number of mortgages are not officially registered (except between the upper castes in Village 3). In this context, the provisions in the act are rather ineffective.[15] Mortgage loans are obtained by underprivileged borrowers from upper class moneylenders mostly on verbal agreements and the borrower being in a weaker position has practically no chance to prove his ownership rights and initiate legal action to recover his land. Besides, debtors belonging to lower castes are financially handicapped and, therefore, cannot afford to take recourse to expensive and prolonged legal proceedings. The situation in the case area is, therefore, still almost the same as illustrated by Hoffman:

> The only course now open to the owner would be to institute an expensive civic suit to prove his right to the field. This means

14. *Transfer of Property Act 1882*, p. 30.

15. The very few number of registered mortgages could be due to actual legal impediments and uncertainties as well as due to registration charges, which the borrower has to bear. Besides the fact that the borrowers are generally not in favour of time-consuming paper work (most of them are illiterate), a registration compels them to meet other expenses, such as for travelling and accommodation possibly even also a payment of a bribe. On the other hand, the creditor is not at all interested in insisting on a registration.

generally a heavy loan at exorbitant interests, varying from 75% to 150%. For that he would have to mortgage all or the best of his remaining fields to the moneylender. Having no documentary evidence at all, the suit, would as a rule, be decided against him by oral evidence.[16]

Interest Rates of Mortgage Loans

The credit sum per Standard Acre of land differs from village to village as well as within villages. Since such differences are mostly related to caste considerations which determine the bargaining power of the borrower, while the moneylender also attempts to have a hand in fixing the credit sum (depending on his motive and strategy), it can be concluded that the final credit sum per Standard Acre is a combined result of the moneylender's strategy and the bargaining power of the borrower.

Similarly, the interest rate for a mortgage loan, too, is determined by the interaction of creditor's strategy on one hand and the debtor's bargaining power on the other. Consequently, the factor which determines the credit sum also decides the level of interest rate (see Table 3.7).[17] For the purpose of the calculation of interest rates in Table 3.7, debtors belonging to similar castes or caste groups are compiled together according to villages. The average credit sum per Standard Acre of land applicable to these caste groups is taken into account while the credit period is fixed as 5 years in terms of the Chota Nagpur Tenancy Act.

Table 3.7 demonstrates that similar to the credit sums per Standard Acre, the interest rates, too, differ considerably between and within

16. J. Hoffman, A. von Emelen, *Encyclopaedia Mundarica*, 13 Vols., Patna, 1950, p. 2930.

17. The average internal interest return is calculated from the following formula:

$$\frac{d}{(1+r)^1}+\frac{d}{(1+r)^2}+\frac{d}{(1+r)^3}+\frac{d}{(1+r)^4}+\frac{d}{(1+r)^5}-k=0$$

where:

d: Difference between Production Return and Production Input per Year per StA

k: Capital borrowed per StA

r: Internal rate of return

Conversion of areas into StA enables to use a uniform net return of 45 Maunds per StA. This is valued at a daily price of Rs 20/- per Maund of Paddy. Production costs are fixed at Rs 253/- per StA on the basis of calculations of Haensch. H. Haensch, "Der Einfluss von betriebswirtschaftlichen, sozialen und versorgungsbedingten Strukturelementen sowie Betriebsleitermerkmalen beim Uebergang zu verbesserten Anbaumethoden in der Landwirtschaft, gezeigt am Beispiel ausgewaehlter Doerfer des Dhanbad-Distriktes, Bihar, Indien", unveroeff. Manuskript, Stuttgart 1976, p. 44.

TABLE 3.7

Average Internal Rate of Interest for Mortgage Loans of Traditional Moneylenders at a Credit Term of Five Years, Classified according to Villages, Castes and/or Caste-Groups

	Debtor: Scheduled Castes, Muslims* / Creditor: Scheduled Castes, Scheduled Tribes, Muslims*	Debtor: Scheduled Castes, Scheduled Tribes / Creditor: Upper Castes, Baniyas**	Debtor: Backward Castes / Creditor: Backward Castes	Debtor: Backward Castes / Creditor: Upper Castes, Baniyas**	Debtor: Upper Castes / Creditor: Backward Castes	Debtor: Upper Castes / Creditor: Upper Castes
Village 1	147.4%	—	47.0%	45.0%	25.9%	—
Village 2	58.1%	67.2%	45.7%	47.8%	—	—
Village 3	85.3%	50.6%	—	—	—	25.1%

Remarks : *Credit Transactions between Muslim Creditors and Debtors have taken place only in Village 1.

**The household belonging to the merchant caste (Baniya) indicated above under Creditor refers to a single Moneylender, who is also the Mukhiya of Village 2.

Source: Own Surveys.

villages. Village 3 has the lowest rate of 25.1%, while the highest rate of 147.4% is levied in Village 1. The rates are, therefore, within almost the same range of interest rates for personal loans mentioned earlier.

An analysis of interest rates in terms of caste relationships indicates that the rates are much higher for credit transactions between backward caste debtors and creditors as well as between these debtors and Muslim moneylenders. This applies especially to Villages 1 and 3. Though the creditor and debtor both belong to similar castes and apparently having equal bargaining powers, the moneylender is somehow still able to enforce his strategy to earn the maximum possible interest. The interest rates charged by upper caste moneylenders from backward caste clients in Villages 2 and 3 are moderate. Although the debtors have a relatively weaker bargaining power, the rates are not as high as can be expected since the moneylenders are primarily motivated to achieve indirect benefits rather than earning direct income returns.

The average interest rates for mortgage loans between backward castes in Villages 1 and 2 as well as between backward castes and traders belonging to the Baniya caste in Village 2 range from 45.7% to 47.8%. The rates are relatively low since the moneylenders are interested in using the lands. Besides, both creditors and debtors belong to similar castes, therefore, due to their balanced bargaining power the moneylenders are unable to demand higher interest rates.

The lowest interest rates are charged for loans between upper caste creditors and backward caste debtors in Village 1 as well as between upper castes in Village 3. The rates vary from 25.1% to 25.9%. The low interest rates are due to the strong negotiating position of debtors. In Village 2, solidarity among upper caste households is powerful, which could have also effectively improved their negotiating position in credit transactions.

It can be stated that although the bargaining powers of creditors and debtors belonging to low castes are presumed to be equal, this is not so in reality. The strategy of the moneylender is the decisive element in fixing the credit sum in these transactions and consequently also the interest rate. However, in credit transactions involving medium (backward) caste households both factors effectively influence the credit sum and interest rate. Such transactions normally carry moderate interest rates. In mortgage loans obtained by upper caste households, the credit sum per Standard Acre is fixed at a higher level with a correspondingly low interest rate due to the high social status and strong negotiating position of the debtors. They get a 'caste bonus' for mortgage loans mainly because of these considerations.

Mortgage of Lands : A Result of a Defective Institutional Credit System[18]

The financing of domestic needs, we have seen, is one of the main reasons for obtaining loans on land mortgages. In Village 1, for instance, most of the loans are for this purpose, except loans obtained for the conversion of cooperative credits, which account for 13.2% of all mortgage transactions. Other credit purposes are rather insignificant (see Table 3.1).

The fact that farmers often mortgage their lands to traditional moneylenders in order to obtain loans to settle cooperative credits is very important. The resulting debt liabilities are due to the defects and weaknesses of the institutional credit system. It was found during our survey that the credit cooperative in Village 1 stopped functioning as a result of the serious drought in 1966-67. Nearly 80% of loans given in 1966 were for consumption and most of these loans could not be recovered. The debtors defaulted paying their loans because of heavy income losses due to crop failures. However, the cooperative officials continued their efforts to recover the loans from the defaulters; the climax of their efforts was reached during the annual 'loan collection campaign'. This was done in spite of the fact that the particular area had already been officially declared as a 'drought area'. Under these circumstances some helpless and ignorant farmers were forced to borrow from the village moneylender to settle their cooperative loans in order to escape from the continued harassments of the cooperative officials. This is only one instance where the institutional credit system, initially established to protect the peasants from the grip of the moneylenders by breaking their monopoly, not only failed but functioned directly against these objectives. We cannot blame only the lower level officials for a misconceived credit policy which resulted in the above situation but more so the upper and medium class decision-makers who are mainly responsible for the fundamental mistakes and negligence. An institutional credit system which is not flexible enough to react in a suitable manner during emergencies, such as droughts and crop failures, forces the debtors to depend again on moneylenders and thereby casts doubts on its own objectives.

Summary

The preceding account is a detailed analysis of the traditional credit market where the main issues are the traditional village moneylender and his business practices.

18. This section deals mainly with Village 1, since there is a strong and direct link between traditional title mortgages and institutional credits in this village.

The potential to produce an agricultural surplus in the case villages was discussed first. It was pointed out that the basis for a surplus production is very much related to the unequal land distribution and also unequal opportunities to earn supplementary off-farm incomes, mainly due to caste and educational differences. Thus, the traditional credit market is dominated by large scale farmers-cum-moneylenders who also occupy key positions in rural administrative bodies. Bihari landowners and traders, who initially migrated during the 19th century played a major role in village credit markets. Comparing the agricultural surplus invested in farm operations and in moneylending, it has been demonstrated that moneylending is a very attractive form of investment for surplus farmers.

In spite of favourable marketing possibilities for agricultural products in the case area, no significant development in agriculture has taken place due to the peculiar situation of agriculture in this area. The agricultural sector consists of two sub-sectors, one made up of farms belonging to the surplus sector and the other consisting of farms in the deficit sector. Deficit farms are characterised by partially regular and partially sporadic credit needs. This creates classic conditions under which surplus farmers invest their agricultural surplus earnings lucratively in the lending business to meet the consumption credit needs of the deficit sector. Moneylending provides attractive avenues to earn above average direct and indirect profits in the form of high interest returns and underpaid or unpaid labour. This precludes any change in the investment pattern of farmers-cum-moneylenders and impedes agricultural development. The investment pattern of large-scale farmers, therefore, is similar to that of dominant landholders of the colonial era. Given the conditions prevailing in the case area no significant development of the agriculture can be expected for a long time.

We concluded that the traditional credit market in the case area is composed of a multitude of smaller, regionally limited markets. Within this limited range of operations, the moneylender has, because of his traditional status and power, effective means to seize the harvest, labour and land of the debtor. By restricting his transactions to a locally limited circle of debtors, the moneylender is able to reduce the risk of delinquency considerably.

An analysis of the traditional credit market form on the basis of the morphological structure of the credit supply has shown that the degree of potential as well as active competition is very low. Consequently, there is almost no competition between traditional moneylenders on one hand and moneylenders and credit cooperatives on the other hand. In Village 2 the elimination of competition has taken place by deliberately blocking underprivileged farm workers from becoming members of the credit cooperative, while in Village 3 the functioning of the cooperative agricultural credit system has been wilfully paralysed. The low mobility of demand has considerably reduced, or even eliminated, competition between lenders operating in the same market. The very low mobility of demand has established conditions which are ideal to create social obligations and dependencies in the case villages where various forms of bonded labour have remained unchanged since the early 19th century.

It is clear that the motive behind private moneylending is primarily to create social obligations rather than to gain direct profits from interest payments. This objective is achieved by exploiting agricultural labourers-cum-debtors who are underpaid or even unpaid. The management of debt transactions as instanced by the mechanisms of debt-farming gives ample evidence of this kind of exploitation. This applies particularly to villages where the tribal social structure was displaced and superseded by a Hindu social order which imposed social subordination. These villages are still characterised by traditional forms of feudal labour. Hence, it should be stressed that interest charges are of only minor relevance and play at best a symbolic part in the moneylending business. All the more important is the moneylenders' management of debts. Because of their overwhelmingly powerful position in the villages and their intimate local and private influence, they are not only in a position to seize whatever exists above the debtor's subsistence level, but also to force him into bondage.

The monopoly of moneylenders is also reflected in their ability to collect exorbitant interest charges, which are very high compared to overall Indian standards. The interest rates and the considerations on which the rates are calculated have not changed over a period of nearly 150 years. This is particularly evident from interest rates charged for loans in kind, which are charged at uniform scales and have become practically institutionalised in the area under survey.

The analysis of different determinant factors and the effect of these factors on the level of interest rates showed clearly that the factor of Monopoly Profit is more decisive and important than other factors such as Opportunity Cost, Administration Cost, and Risk Cost. Considering the traditional behaviour patterns of an agricultural society and particularly in view of the market form and the degree of mobility of demand (and hence the type of competition) this was to be expected. The characteristic power patterns of an underdeveloped agricultural society thus provide ideal conditions to achieve very high direct and indirect profits from moneylending.

Mortgage loans are, relatively speaking, important in the credit transactions of traditional moneylenders. Nearly one-third of their loan activities are based on mortgages, indicating the aspiration of the moneylender to minimise the risk of delinquency. Heavy credit demands to cover family expenses and increasing shortage of land have resulted in different forms of land mortgages.

The interaction between the moneylender's strategy and the bargaining power of the debtor leads to various repayment modes and loan agreements. Underprivileged castes are usually in a weaker position to negotiate a credit transaction and due to their ignorance of legal aspects they are adversely affected by the credit formalities of moneylenders. Because of these disadvantages, they are often unable to redeem the mortgages and lose their land. The final result of these mortgages is that the already existing uncontrolled changeover of land from poor to rich is further intensified creating greater disparities in the agriculture of the case area.

Appendix

TABLE A1

Distribution of the Overall Credit Volume and the Credit Sources in the Case Villages during the Period 1966-67—1971-72 (in Rupees)

Village/ farm size class (in StA)	Total house-holds	Credit volume per house-hold	Credit volume per house-hold per year	(1) C.D. Block		(2) Coopera-tive		(3) Land Mortgage Bank		(4) Village Moneylenders: Inner circle		(5) Village Moneylenders: Outer circle		(6) Friends/ Relatives		(7) Misc.*		(8) Total	
				Amt.	%	Amt.	%	Amt.	%	Amt.	%	Amt.	%	Amt.	%	Amt.	%	Amt.	%
1	2	3	4	5	6	7	8	9	10	11	12	13	14	15	16	17	18	19	20
Village 1																			
Under 2.0	26	812.5	135.4	330	1.6	2,180	10.3	—	—	8,947	42.4	6,327	29.9	3,095	14.6	246	1.2	21,125	100
2.01— 5.0	27	1,418.0	236.3	1,643	4.3	1,010	2.6	—	—	10,490	27.4	21,784	56.9	3,290	8.6	70	0.2	38,287	100
5.01—10.0	5	236.3	47.3	730	6.2	350	3.0	—	—	5,070	42.9	3,850	32.6	1,715	14.5	100	0.8	11,815	100
Over 10.0	1	—	—	—	—	—	—	—	—	—	—	—	—	—	—	—	—	—	—
Sub-total 1	59	1,207.2	201.2	2,703	3.8	3,540	5.0	—	—	24,507	34.4	31,961	44.8	8,100	11.4	416	0.6	71,227	100
Village 2																			
Under 2.0	26	528.8	88.1	2,290**	16.7	2,975	21.6	—	—	2,600	18.9	885	6.4	3,690	26.9	1,310	26.9	13,750	100
2.01— 5.0	3	993.3	165.5	30	1.0	1,300	43.6	—	—	1,000	33.6	300	10.0	270	9.1	80	2.7	2,980	100
5.01—10.0	—	—	—	—	—	—	—	—	—	—	—	—	—	—	—	—	—	—	—
Over 10.0	1	300.0	50.0	300	100.0	—	—	—	—	—	—	—	—	—	—	—	—	300	100
Sub-total 2	30	567.7	94.6	2,260	15.4	4,275	25.1	—	—	3,600	21.1	1,185	7.0	3,960	23.3	1,390	8.1	17,030	100

(contd.)

(*contd. A1*)

1	2	3	4	5	6	7	8	9	10	11	12	13	14	15	16	17	18	19	20
Village 3																			
Under 2.0	10	335.0	55.8	100	3.0	600	17.9	—	—	1,890	56.4	640	19.1	120	3.6	—	—	3,350	100
2.01— 5.0	11	1,226.6	204.4	683	5.1	600	4.4	—	—	3,560	26.4	300	2.2	4,650	34.5	3,700	27.4	13,493	100
5.01—10.0	7	4,769.6	794.9	1,815	5.4	2,960	8.9	5,000	15.0	2,860	8.5	12,752	38.2	7,500	22.5	500	1.5	33,387	100
Over 10.0	3	5,097.3	849.6	2,052	13.4	2,600	17.0	—	—	—	—	1,100	7.2	9,450	62.4	—	—	15,292	100
Sub-total 3	31	2,113.6	352.3	4,650	7.1	6,760	10.3	5,000	7.6	8,310	12.7	14,792	22.6	21,810	33.3	4,200	6.4	65,522	100
Full total	120	1,281.5	213.6	9,973	6.5	14,575	9.5	5,000	3.2	36,417	23.7	47,938	31.2	33,870	22.0	6,006	3.9	153,779	100

Remarks : *Items mentioned under 'Misc.' in regard to Village 1 and Village 2 are credits given by Shopkeepers and small loans of Madrasi-Moneylenders. In respect of Village 3 the items under 'Misc.' are Provident Fund loans. Since these credits are only single cases, a separate classification has not been done.

**Out of this amount of Rs. 2290, Rs. 2000 is a credit given to a 'Contractor', who has been instructed to construct a school building in the village from these funds. However, the debtor has misappropriated the credit by using it to finance the marriage of his son.

Source: Own Surveys.

TABLE A2

Financing Pattern of Land Purchases in the Case Villages during the Period 1966-67—1971-72
(in Rupees)

Village/ farm-size class (in StA)	(1) Sale of land and livestock		(2) Savings, dowries, sale of jewellery		(3) Sale of farm products		(4) Off-farm incomes w.o. 5 & 6		(5) Employment in public service		(6) Handicrafts, trade and services		(7) Institutional credits		(8) Traditional credits		(9) Total	
	Amt.	%	Amt.	%	Amt.	%	Amt.	%	Amt.	%	Amt.	%	Amt.	%	Amt.	%	Amt.	%
1	2	3	4	5	6	7	8	9	10	11	12	13	14	15	16	17	18	19
Village 1																		
Under 2.0	1,150	22.7	3,130	61.6	—	—	500	09.8	—	—	—	—	—	—	300	05.9	5,080	100
2.01— 5.0	860	6.5	1,090	8.3	—	—	1,000	7.6	4,680	35.5	—	—	—	—	5,560	42.1	13,190	100
5.01—10.0	450	21.2	—	—	50	02.3	—	—	—	—	—	—	—	—	1,628	76.5	2,128	100
Over 10.0	200	40.0	—	—	300	60.0	—	—	—	—	—	—	—	—	—	—	500	100
Total	2,660	12.7	4,220	20.2	350	01.7	1,500	07.2	4,680	22.4	—	—	—	—	7,488	35.8	20,898	100
Village 2																		
Under 2.0	200	05.2	1,000	26.3	—	—	—	—	200	05.3	1,500	39.5	—	—	900	23.7	3,800	100
2.01— 5.0	—	—	—	—	—	—	—	—	400	100.0	—	—	—	—	—	—	400	100
5.01—10.0	—	—	—	—	—	—	—	—	—	—	—	—	—	—	—	—	—	—
Over 10.0	—	—	5,000	83.3	1,000	16,7	—	—	—	—	—	—	—	—	—	—	6,000	100
Total	200	02.0	6,000	58.8	1,000	09.8	—	—	600	05.9	1,500	14.7	—	—	900	08.8	10,200	100

(*contd.*)

(*contd. A2*)

1	2	3	4	5	6	7	8	9	10	11	12	13	14	15	16	17	18	19
Village 3																		
Under 2.0	—	—	200	100.0	—	—	—	—	—	—	—	—	—	—	—	—	200	100
2.01— 5.0	—	—	—	—	—	—	200	100.0	—	—	—	—	—	—	—	—	200	100
5.01—10.0	—	—	—	—	400	16.7	—	—	1,600	66.6	400	16.7	—	—	—	—	2,400	100
Over 10.0	—	—	—	—	500	100.0	—	—	—	—	—	—	—	—	—	—	500	100
Total	—	—	200	06.1	900	27.2	200	06.1	1,600	48.5	400	12.1	—	—	—	—	3,300	100
Full Total	2,860	08.3	10,420	30.3	2,250	06.6	1,700	04.9	6,880	20.0	1,900	05.5	—	—	8,388	24.4	34,398	100

Source : Own Surveys.

TABLE A3

Financing Pattern of Livestock (Cattle) Purchases in the Case Villages during the Period 1966-67—1971-72 (in Rupees)

	(1)		(2)		(3)		(4)		(5)		(6)		(7)		(8)		(9)	
Village/ farm-size class (in StA)	Sale of land and livestock		Savings, dowries sale of jewellery		Sale of farm products		Off-farm incomes w.o. 5 & 6		Employ-ment in public service		Handi-crafts, trade and services		Institu-tional credits		Tradi-tional credits		Total	
	Amt.	%	Amt.	%	Amt.	%	Amt.	%	Amt.	%	Amt.	%	Amt.	%	Amt.	%	Amt.	%
1	2	3	4	5	6	7	8	9	10	11	12	13	14	15	16	17	18	19
Village 1																		
Under 2.0	1,095	32.9	—	—	93	02.8	1,158	34.7	—	—	—	—	—	—	—	29.6	3,331	100
2.01— 5.0	2,383	31.1	800	10.4	177	02.3	1,509	19.7	60	00.8	300	03.9	400	05.2	2,040	26.6	7,669	100
5.01—10.0	590	33.8	—	—	445	25.5	410	23.5	—	—	—	—	200	11.5	100	05.7	1,745	100
Over 10.0	—	—	—	—	—	—	—	—	—	—	—	—	—	—	—	—	—	—
Total	4,068	31.9	800	06.3	715	05.6	3,077	24.1	60	00.5	300	02.4	600	04.7	3,125	24.5	12,745	100
Village 2																		
Under 2.0	560	23.8	200	08.5	240	10.2	200	08.5	—	—	750	31.9	300	12.8	100	04.3	2,350	100
2.01— 5.0	—	—	—	—	—	—	—	—	—	—	450	100	—	—	—	—	450	100
5.01—10.0	—	—	—	—	—	—	—	—	—	—	—	—	—	—	—	—	—	—
Over 10.0	—	—	—	—	—	—	—	—	—	—	600	100	—	—	—	—	600	100
Total	560	16.5	200	05.9	240	07.1	200	05.9	—	—	1,800	52.9	300	08.8	100	02.9	3,400	100

(contd.)

(*contd. A3*)

1	2	3	4	5	6	7	8	9	10	11	12	13	14	15	16	17	18	19
Village 3																		
Under 2.0	—	—	—	—	70	12.2	—	—	—	—	—	—	200	34.8	305	53.0	575	100
2.01— 5.0	400	31.3	—	—	170	13.3	60	04.7	300	23.4	250	19.5	100	07.8	—	—	1,280	100
5.01—10.0	300	07.5	—	—	1,500	37.6	—	—	840	21.1	—	—	950	23.8	400	10.0	3,990	100
Over 10.0	—	—	—	—	—	—	—	—	—	—	—	—	1,700	81.1	400	19.0	2,100	100
Total	700	08.8	—	—	1,740	21.9	60	00.8	1,140	14.4	250	03.1	2,950	37.1	1,105	13.9	7,945	100
Full Total	5,328	22.1	1,000	04.1	2,695	11.2	3,377	13.8	1,200	05.0	2,350	09.8	3,850	16.0	4,330	18.0	24,090	100

Source : Own Surveys.

TABLE A4

Financing Pattern of Investment in Land Improvement and Irrigation in the Case Villages during the Period 1966-67—1971-72 (in Rupees)

Villages/ farm-size class (in StA)	(1) Sale of land and livestock		(2) Savings, dowries, sale of jewellery		(3) Sale of farm products		(4) Off-farm incomes w.o. 5 & 6		(5) Employment in public service		(6) Handicrafts, trade and services		(7) Institutional credits		(8) Traditional credits		(9) Disposal of own labour		(10) Total	
	Amt.	%	Amt.	%	Amt.	%	Amt.	%	Amt.	%	Amt.	%	Amt.	%	Amt.	%	Amt.	%	Amt.	%
1	2	3	4	5	6	7	8	9	10	11	12	13	14	15	16	17	18	19	20	21
Village 1																				
Under 2.0	200	10.2	—	—	—	—	600	30.6	—	—	60	03.1	—	—	200	10.2	900	45.9	1,960	100
2.01— 5.0	—	—	—	—	160	04.1	—	—	—	—	—	—	—	—	430	11.1	3,274	84.8	3,864	100
5.01—10 0	—	—	—	—	640	23.4	—	—	—	—	70	02.6	730	26.6	300	10.9	1,000	36.5	2,740	100
Over 10.0	—	—	—	—	—	—	—	—	—	—	—	—	—	—	—	—	—	—	—	—
Total	200	02.3	—	—	800	09.3	600	30.6	—	—	130	01.5	730	08.6	930	10 9	5,174	60.4	8,564	100
Village 2																				
Under 2.0	—	—	—	—	—	—	—	—	100	04.0	150	06.0	100	04.4	—	—	2,150	86.0	2,500	100
2.01— 5.0	—	—	—	—	—	—	—	—	—	—	—	—	—	—	—	—	—	—	—	—
5.01—10.0	—	—	—	—	—	—	—	—	—	—	—	—	—	—	—	—	—	—	—	—
Over 10.0	—	—	—	—	200	25.0	—	—	—	—	600	75.0	—	—	—	—	—	—	800	100
Total	—	—	—	—	200	06.1	—	—	100	03.3	750	22.7	100	03.3	—	—	2,150	65.2	3,300	100

(contd.)

(*contd. A4*)

1	2	3	4	5	6	7	8	9	10	11	12	13	14	15	16	17	18	19	20	21
Village 3																				
Under 2.0	—	—	—	—	—	—	—	—	—	—	—	—	—	—	—	—	100	100.0	100	100
2.01— 5.0	—	—	—	—	—	—	—	—	700	63.6	—	—	300	27.3	—	—	100	09.1	1,100	100
5.01—10.0	—	—	—	—	1,300	17.3	—	—	300	04.0	—	—	5,900	78.7	—	—	—	—	7,500	100
Over 10.0	—	—	—	—	1,350	29.4	—	—	200	04.3	—	—	2,850	62.0	—	—	200	04.3	4,600	100
Total	—	—	—	—	2,650	19.9	—	—	1,200	09.0	—	—	9,050	68.1	—	—	400	03.0	13,300	100
Full Total	200	00.8	—	—	3,650	14.5	600	02.4	1,300	05.1	880	03.5	9,880	39.3	930	03.7	7,724	30.7	25,164	100

Source : Own Surveys.

TABLE A5

Financing Pattern of the Expenditure Incurred in Constructing Dwelling Houses, Stalls and Repair/Maintenance of Buildings in the Case Villages during the Period 1966-67—1971-72 (in Rupees)

Villages/ farm-size class (in StA)	(1) Sale of land and livestock		(2) Savings, dowries, sale of jewellery		(3) Sale of farm products		(4) Off-farm incomes w.o. 5 & 6		(5) Employment in public service		(6) Handicrafts, trade and services		(7) Institutional credits		(8) Traditional credits		(9) Disposal of own labour		(10) Total	
	Amt.	%	Amt.	%	Amt.	%	Amt.	%	Amt.	%	Amt.	%	Amt.	%	Amt.	%	Amt.	%	Amt.	%
1	2	3	4	5	6	7	8	9	10	11	12	13	14	15	16	17	18	19	20	21
Village 1																				
Under 2.0	170	02.3	1,110	15.2	30	00.4	1,980	27.2	240	03.3	1,535	21.1	90	01.2	630	08.7	1,500	20.6	7,291	100
2.01— 5.0	1,950	18.2	1,200	11.2	350	03.3	2,503	23.4	820	07.7	150	01.4	—	—	830	07.8	2,890	27.0	10,693	100
5.01—10.0	—	—	300	08.5	1,657	46.7	610	17.2	—	—	—	—	—	—	980	27.6	—	—	3,547	100
Over 10.0	—	—	—	—	55	26.8	150	73.2	—	—	—	—	—	—	—	—	—	—	205	100
Total	2,120	09.8	2,610	12.0	2,092	09.6	5,249	24.1	1,060	04.9	1,685	07.8	90	00.4	2,440	11.2	4,390	20.2	21,736	100
Village 2																				
Under 2.0	—	—	—	—	100	01.8	680	12.3	860	15.5	2,706	48.9	300	05.4	690	12.5	200	03.6	5,536	100
2.01— 5.0	—	—	—	—	159	24.0	—	—	—	—	75	12.0	300	48.0	—	—	100	16.0	634	100
5.01—10.0	—	—	—	—	—	—	—	—	—	—	—	—	—	—	—	—	—	—	—	—
Over 10.0	—	—	—	—	—	—	—	—	—	—	1,100	100.0	—	—	—	—	—	—	1,100	100
Total	—	—	—	—	249	03.5	680	09.4	860	11.8	3,881	53.4	600	08.3	690	09.5	300	04.1	7,270	100

(contd.)

(contd. A5)

1	2	3	4	5	6	7	8	9	10	11	12	13	14	15	16	17	18	19	20	21
Village 3																				
Under 2.0	—	—	—	—	—	—	430	89.6	50	10.4	—	—	—	—	—	—	—	—	480	100
2.01— 5.0	—	—	—	—	100	02.6	840	21.8	1,750	45.3	580	15.0	—	—	—	—	590	15.3	3,860	100
5.01—10.0	—	—	3,500	45.6	1,575	20.5	—	—	2,600	33.9	—	—	—	—	—	—	—	—	7,675	100
Over 10.0	—	—	—	—	500	45.0	—	—	10	00.9	600	54.1	—	—	—	—	—	—	1,110	100
Total	—	—	3,500	26.7	2,175	16.6	1,270	09.7	4,410	33.6	1,180	09.0	—	—	—	—	590	04.4	13,125	100
Full Total	2,120	05.0	6,110	14.5	4,526	10.7	7,199	17.1	6,330	15 0	6,746	16.0	690	01.6	3,130	07.5	5,280	12.6	42,131	100

Source : Own Surveys.

TABLE A6

Financing Pattern of Domestic Events (Marriages, Funerals) during the Period 1966-67—1971-72
(in Rupees)

Village/ farm-size class (in StA)	(1) Sale of land and livestock		(2) Savings, dowries, sale of jewellery		(3) Sale of farm products		(4) Off-farm incomes w.o. 5 & 6		(5) Employment in public service		(6) Handicrafts, trade and services		(7) Institutional credits		(8) Traditional credits		(9) Total	
	Amt.	%	Amt.	%	Amt.	%	Amt.	%	Amt.	%	Amt.	%	Amt.	%	Amt.	%	Amt.	%
1	2	3	4	5	6	7	8	9	10	11	12	13	14	15	16	17	18	19
Village 1																		
Under 2.0	3,075	18.7	900	05.5	300	01.8	1,950	11.9	260	01.6	225	01.4	1,025	06.3	8,650	52.8	16,385	100
2.01— 5.0	3,300	11.1	2,890	09.7	1,920	06.4	1,250	04.2	1,040	03.5	750	02.5	—	—	18,700	62.6	29,850	100
5.01—10.0	230	02.3	—	—	5,400	54.2	—	—	—	—	—	—	—	—	4,335	43.5	9,965	100
Over 10.0	—	—	1,500	50.0	1,500	—	—	—	—	—	—	—	—	—	—	—	3,000	100
Total	6,605	11.2	5,290	08.9	9,120	15.4	3,200	05.4	1,300	02.2	975	01.6	1,025	01.7	31,685	53.6	59,200	100
Village 2																		
Under 2.0	1,500	08.9	3,260	19.3	480	02.8	—	—	300	01.8	3,840	22.7	2,750	16.3	4,750	28.2	16,880	100
2.01— 5.0	—	—	1,500	38.0	200	05.1	—	—	—	—	900	22.8	—	—	1,350	34.1	3,950	100
5.01—10.0	—	—	—	—	—	—	—	—	—	—	—	—	—	—	—	—	—	—
Over 10.0	—	—	6,000	100.0	—	—	—	—	—	—	—	—	—	—	—	—	6,000	100
Total	1,500	05.6	10,760	40.1	680	02.5	—	—	300	01.1	4,740	17.7	2,750	10.3	6,100	22.7	26,830	100

(contd.)

(contd. A6)

1	2	3	4	5	6	7	8	9	10	11	12	13	14	15	16	17	18	19
Village 3																		
Under 2.0	120	05.3	—	—	90	04.0	400	17.8	—	—	—	—	200	08.9	1,440	64.0	2,250	100
2.01— 5.0	3,000	16.8	250	01.4	250	01.4	600	03.4	2,300	12.9	150	00.8	—	—	11,320	63.3	17,870	100
5.01—10.0	1,000	03.4	7,500	25.3	500	01.7	200	00.7	—	—	—	—	800	02.7	19,660	66.2	29,660	100
Over 10.0	—	—	5,500	28.0	—	—	—	—	1,900	09.7	2,000	10.2	—	—	10,240	52.1	19,640	100
Total	4,120	05.9	13,250	19.1	840	01.2	1,200	01.7	4,200	06.1	2,150	03.1	1,000	01.4	42,660	61.5	69,420	100
Full Total	12,225	07.9	29,300	18.8	10,640	06.8	4,400	02.8	5,800	03.7	7,865	05.1	4,775	03.1	80,445	51.8	155,450	100

Source : Own Surveys.

TABLE A7

Financing Pattern of Expenditure Incurred on Education and Medical Attention during the Period 1966-67—1971-72

(in Rupees)

Village/ farm-size class (in StA)	(1) Sale of land and livestock		(2) Savings, dowries, sale of jewellery		(3) Sale of farm products		(4) Off-farm incomes w.o. 5 & 6		(5) Employ-ment in public service		(6) Handi-crafts, trade and services		(7) Institu-tional credits		(8) Tradi-tional credits		(9) Total	
	Amt.	%	Amt.	%	Amt.	%	Amt.	%	Amt.	%	Amt.	%	Amt.	%	Amt.	%	Amt.	%
1	2	3	4	5	6	7	8	9	10	11	12	13	14	15	16	17	18	19
Village 1																		
Under 2.0	92	09.8	—	—	85	09.1	365	39.0	—	—	245	26.1	20	02.1	130	13.9	937	100
2.01— 5.0	—	—	—	—	157	11.2	260	18.5	390	27.7	160	11.4	50	03.5	390	27.7	1,407	100
5.01—10.0	—	—	—	—	145	26.2	110	19.8	—	—	100	18.0	—	—	200	36.0	555	100
Over 10.0	—	—	—	—	—	—	20	—	—	—	—	—	—	—	—	—	20	100
Total	92	03.1	—	—	387	13.2	755	25.9	390	13.4	505	17.3	70	02.4	720	24.7	2,919	100
Village 2																		
Under 2 0	—	—	—	—	75	06.1	—	—	185	15.0	75	06.1	—	—	900	72.8	1,235	100
2.01— 5.0	—	—	900	39.1	200	39.1	—	—	—	—	900	39.1	300	13.1	—	—	2,300	100
5.01—10.0	—	—	—	—	—	—	—	—	—	—	—	—	—	—	—	—	—	—
Over 10.0	—	—	—	—	400	—	—	—	—	—	1,000	71.4	—	—	—	—	1,400	100
Total	—	—	900	18.2	675	13.7	—	—	185	03.8	1,975	40.0	300	06.1	900	18.2	4,935	100

(contd.)

(*contd. A7*)

1	2	3	4	5	6	7	8	9	10	11	12	13	14	15	16	17	18	19
Village 3																		
Under 2.0	—	—	—	—	—	—	15	100.0	—	—	—	—	—	—	—	—	15	100
2.01— 5.0	—	—	—	—	—	—	350	20,0	1,000	57.1	340	19.4	—	—	60	03.5	1,750	100
5.01—10.0	—	—	—	—	900	28.1	80	02.5	1,820	56.9	—	—	—	—	400	12.5	3,200	100
Over 10.0	—	—	—	—	1,700	94.4	—	—	100	05.6	—	—	—	—	—	—	1,800	100
Total	—	—	—	—	2,600	38.4	445	06.6	2,920	43.2	340	05.5	—	—	460	06.8	6,765	100
Full Total	92	00.6	900	06.2	3,662	25.1	1,200	08.2	3,495	23.9	2,820	19.3	370	02.5	2,080	14.2	14,619	100

Source : Own Surveys.

TABLE A8

Financing Pattern of Expenditure Incurred on Legal Proceedings during the Period 1966-67—1971-72

(in Rupees)

Village/ farm-size class (in StA)	(1) Sale of land and livestock		(2) Savings, dowries, sale of jewellery		(3) Sale of farm products		(4) Off-farm incomes w.o. 5 & 6		(5) Employment in public service		(6) Handicrafts, trade and services		(7) Institutional credits		(8) Traditional credits		(9) Total	
	Amt.	%	Amt.	%	Amt.	%	Amt.	%	Amt.	%	Amt.	%	Amt.	%	Amt.	%	Amt.	%
1	2	3	4	5	6	7	8	9	10	11	12	13	14	15	16	17	18	19
Village 1																		
Under 2.0	—	—	800	33.4	—	—	1,200	50.0	—	—	—	—	200	08.3	200	08.3	2,400	100
2.01— 5.0	700	92.1	—	—	60	07.9	—	—	—	—	—	—	—	—	—	—	760	100
5.01—10.0	—	—	—	—	—	—	—	—	—	—	—	—	—	—	850	100.0	850	100
Over 10.0	—	—	—	—	—	—	—	—	—	—	—	—	—	—	—	—	—	—
Total	700	17.5	800	19.9	60	01.5	1,200	29.9	—	—	—	—	200	05.0	1,050	26.2	4,010	100
Village 2																		
Under 5.0	—	—	—	—	—	—	—	—	—	—	—	—	—	—	300	100.0	300	100
2.01— 5.0	—	—	—	—	—	—	—	—	—	—	—	—	—	—	—	—	—	—
5·01—10.0	—	—	—	—	—	—	—	—	—	—	—	—	—	—	—	—	—	—
Over 10.0	—	—	—	—	—	—	—	—	—	—	—	—	—	—	—	—	—	—
Total	—	—	—	—	—	—	—	—	—	—	—	—	—	—	300	100.0	300	100

(contd.)

(*contd. A8*)

1	2	3	4	5	6	7	8	9	10	11	12	13	14	15	16	17	18	19
Village 3																		
Under 2.0	—	—	—	—	—	—	—	—	—	—	—	—	—	—	—	—	—	—
2.01— 5.0	—	—	—	—	—	—	—	—	—	—	—	—	—	—	—	—	—	—
5.01—10.0	—	—	—	—	750	31.3	150	06.2	—	—	—	—	500	20.8	1,000	41.7	2,400	100
Over 10.0	—	—	—	—	2,000	100.0	—	—	—	—	—	—	—	—	—	—	2,000	100
Total	—	—	—	—	2,750	62.5	150	03.4	—	—	—	—	500	11.4	1,000	22.7	4,400	100
Full Total	700	08.8	800	09.2	2,810	32.3	1,350	15.5	—	—	—	—	700	08.0	2,350	27.0	8,710	100

Source : Own Surveys.

Bibliography

Bottomly, A., "Monopoly Profit as a Determinant of Interest Rates in Underdeveloped Rural Areas" in *Oxford Economic Papers*, Vol. 16, No. 3 (October 1964).

Bottomly, A., "The Premium for Risk as a Determinant of Interest Rates in Underdeveloped Rural Areas" in *The Quarterly Journal of Economics*, Vol. 77, No. 4 (November 1963).

Bottomly, A., "The Cost of Administering Private Loans in Underdeveloped Areas" in Shukla, T. (ed.), *Economics of Underdeveloped Agriculture*, Bombay, 1969.

Bottomly, A., "Reply" in *The Quarterly Journal of Economics*, Vol. 79, No. 2 (May 1965).

Census 1971, Bihar, District Census Handbook, Dhanbad District.

Chandravarkar, A.G., "The Premium for Risk as a Determinant of Interest Rates in Underdeveloped Rural Areas: Comment" in *Quarterly Journal of Economics*, Vol. 72, No. 2 (May 1965).

Dandekar, V.M., "Questions of Economic Analysis and the Consequences of Population Growth: Comment" in Wharton, C.R. (ed.), *Subsistence Agriculture and Economic Development*, Chicago, 1969.

Dandekar, V.M., "Transforming Traditional Agriculture, A Critique of Prof. Schultz" in *Economic and Political Weekly*, August 20, 1966.

Darling, M., *The Punjab Peasant in Prosperity and Debt*, 4th edn., Oxford University Press, 1947.

Datey, C.D., "Cooperative Credit" in *Cooperative News Digest*, Vol. XXV, No. 12, December 1974, Reserve Bank of India, Agricultural Credit Department.

Government of Bihar: Directorate of Statistics and Evaluation, *Annual Season and Crop Report for the Agricultural Years 1961/62 to 1971/72.*

Government of Bihar: Law Department, *The Bihar Moneylenders Act, 1938, (As modified up to the 24th May 1963)*, Patna, 1963.

Government of Bihar, Law Department, *The Chota Nagpur Tenancy Act 1908, (Bihar Act 7 of 1948), as modified up to the 15th November 1965*, Patna, 1966.

Haensch, H., "Der Einfluss von betriebswirtschaftlichen, sozialen und versorgungsbedingten Strukturelementen sowie Betriebsleitermerkmalen beim Uebergang zu verbesserten Anbaumethoden in der Landwirtschaft, gezeigt am Beispiel ausgewaehlter Doerfer des Dhanbad-Distriktes, Bihar, Indien", unveroeff. Manuskript, Stuttgart, 1976.

Hoffman, J., Emelen, A., von, et al., *Encyclopaedia Mundarica*, 13 Vols., Patna, 1950.

Journal of the Royal Asiatic Society of Great Britain and Ireland: Vols. XIII, (1846).

Kiermayer, U., *Kredit im Entwicklungsprozess traditioneller Landwirtschaft in Westpakistan*, Saarbruecken, 1971.

Krelle, W., *Preistheorie*, Tuebingen-Zuerich, 1961.

Kropp, E.W., "Kapitalbildung landwirtschaftlicher Betriebe im Hinterland von Dhanbad, SFB 16, Dhanbad-Projekt", unveroeff. Manuskript, Heidelberg, 1972.

Kropp, E.W., "Landwirtschaftliche Kapitalbildung unter Industrie-Einfluss: Ein empirischer Beitrag zum Spar- und Investitionsverhalten landwirtschaftlicher Haushalte in Indien", unveroeff. Manuskript, Heidelberg, 1976.

Kropp, E.W., Der Einfluss des Bergbaus auf die Beschaeftigungsstruktur in laendlichen Gemeinden, Beitraege zur Suedasienforschung, Suedasien-Institut, Universitaet Heidelberg, Band 19, Wiesbaden, 1976.

Lipton, M., "Agricultural Finance and Rural Credit in Poor Countries" in *World Development*, Vol. 4, No. 7, 1976.

Long, M., "Interest Rates and the Structure of Agricultural Credit Markets" in *Oxford Economic Papers*, Vol. 20, No. 2 (July 1968).

Maharaj, R.N., "Freed Bonded Labour Camp at Palamau" in *National Labour Institute Bulletin*, 10/1976.

Maharaj, R.N., "The Impact of State Policy on Agricultural Development, SFB 16, Dhanbad Projekt", unveroeff. Manuskript, Heidelberg, 1972.

Mukerjee, R., *The Foundation of Indian Economics*, London-New York-Calcutta-Bombay-Madras.

Mundle, S., "The Bonded of Palamau" in *Economic and Political Weekly*, Vol. XI, No. 18, May 1, 1976.

National Council of Applied Economic Research, *Effectiveness of Cooperative Credit for Agricultural Production*, New Delhi, 1972.

National Council of Applied Economic Research, *Techno-Economic Survey of Bihar*, Vol. 1, New Delhi, 1959.

National Survey on the Incidence of Bonded Labour, Preliminary Report, New Delhi, 1979.

Nisbet, Ch. T., "Informal Lenders as Suppliers of Development Credits to Small Farmers in Developing Countries: Attractive or Deceptive Alternative" in *Small Farmer Credit, Informal Credit, A.I.D. Spring Review of Small Farmer Credit*, Vol. XV, No. SR 115, Washington, 1973.

Patnaik, U., "Capitalist Development in Agriculture, A Note" in *Economic and Political Weekly*, Review of Agriculture, Vol. VI, September 25, 1971, pp A/123-A/150.

Prasad, P.H., "Agrarian Unrest and Economic Change in Rural Bihar, Three Case Studies" in *Economic and Political Weekly*, Vol. X, No. 24, June 14, 1975.

Reserve Bank of India, *Report of the Agricultural Finance Sub-Committee, 1945*, Reprinted on behalf of the Government of India, Bombay, 1965.

Reserve Bank of India, *All-India Rural Credit Survey, Vol. II, The Survey Report, Part 2 (Credit Agencies)*, Bombay, 1957.

Reserve Bank of India, *All-India Rural Credit Survey, Vol. II, The General Report*, Bombay, 1954.

Reserve Bank of India, *Land Mortgage Bank*, Bombay, 1951.

Reserve Bank of India, *Report of the All-India Rural Credit Review Committee*, Bombay, 1969.

Reserve Bank of India, "Contribution of Cooperative Credit to Agricultural Development in India" in *Cooperative News Digest*, Vol. XXIV, No. 6, 1973.

Roth, H.D., *Institutioneller Agrarkredit und traditionelle Schuldverhaeltnisse*, Wiesbaden, 1978.

Roth, H.D., "Moneylender's Management of Loan Agreements" in *Economic and Political Weekly*, Vol. XIV, No. 28, July 14, 1979.

Rothermund, D., Wadhwa, D.C. (ed.), *Zamindars, Mines and Peasants*, South Asian Studies, No. IX(a), New Delhi, 1978.

Rudra, A., "Loan as a Part of Agrarian Relations, Some Results of a Preliminary Survey in West Bengal" in *Economic and Political Weekly*, Vol. X, No. 20, July 12, 1965.

Schwerin, D., *Von Armut zu Elend*. Kolonialherrschaft und Agrarverfassung in Chota Nagpur, 1858-1908, Beitraege zur Suedasienforschung, Suedasien-Institut, Universitaet Heidelberg, Bd. 31, Wiesbaden, 1977.

Schultz, Th. W., *Transforming Traditional Agriculture*, New Haven, 1965.

Schmitt, E., "Die bevoelkerungsgeschichtliche Entwicklung im Dhanbad-Distrikt seit der Kolonialisierung," Eine zusammenfassende Darstellung der Detribalisierung, Sonderforschungsbereich 16, Dhanbad-Projekt, unveroeff. Manuskript, Heidelberg, 1974.

Schwerin, D., "Preliminary Draft, Dhanbad-Gesamtbericht", unveroeff. Manuskript, New York, 1976.

Singh, K., "Structural Analysis of Interest Rates on Consumption Loans in an Indian Village" in *Asian Economic Review*, Vol. 10, No. 4, (August 1968).

Sivaswamy, K.G., *The Cooperative Movement in Bihar, A Study in Organisation and Technique*, New Delhi, 1956.

Subramanium, "Co-ops only Alternative to Moneylender?" in *Cooperative News Digest*, Vol. XXVII, No. 12, December 1976.

The Bihar and Orissa Provincial Banking Enquiry Committee: 1929-1930, 3 Volumes, Patna, 1930.

Transfer of Property Act, 1882.

Urff, W., von, et. al., "Wirtschaftliche und soziale Dualismen in einem indischen Bergbaugebiet, dargestellt am Beispiel des Distriktes Dhanbad/Bihar. Eine zusammenfassende Darstellung des Forschungsprojektes, SFB 16", unveroeff. Manuskript, Heidelberg, 1972.

Urff, W. von, et. al., "Zur Durchfuehrbarkeit eines deutsch-indischen Landwirtschaftsprojektes im Distrikt Ranchi (Indien)," Gutachten erstellt im Auftrag des Bundesministeriums fuer wirtschaftliche Zusammenarbeit, Heidelberg, 1974.

Urff, W., von, "Agrarpolitische Probleme der Entwicklungslaender", Vorlesungsmanuskript, Heidelberg, 1972.

Index